I Love Me

AVOIDING & OVERCOMING

DEPRESSION

I Love Me

AVOIDING & OVERCOMING

DEPRESSION

A Practical Guide for:
- **Avoiding & Overcoming Depression**
- **Developing Proper Self-Esteem**
- **Obtaining a Victorious Life with Joy, Substance and Purpose**

DIETMAR SCHERF

SCHERF
BOOKS

DEPRESSION: *Avoiding & Overcoming* • *I Love Me*

ISBN 1-887603-03-4
Library of Congress Catalog Card Number: 97-91343

First Edition

*Grateful acknowledgment is made to the following for permission to reprint
previously published material:* Christian Publications: An excerpt from "The
Best of A.B. Simpson" compiled by Keith M. Bailey. Copyright © 1987 by
Christian Publications. All rights reserved. Reprinted by permission.

"Scripture taken from THE AMPLIFIED BIBLE, Old Testament
copyright © 1965, 1987 by The Zondervan Corporation. The Amplified
New Testament copyright © 1958, 1987 by The Lockman Foundation.
Used by permission." *Whenever Scripture is quoted from this Bible
translation it is indicated with "The Amplified Bible."*

"Scripture taken from the NEW AMERICAN STANDARD BIBLE,
© 1960, 1962, 1963, 1968, 1971, 1972, 1973, 1975, 1977, by The Lockman
Foundation. Used by permission." *Whenever Scripture is quoted from
this Bible translation it is indicated with "NASB."*

*Whenever Scripture is quoted from the King James Version of The Holy
Bible it is indicated with "KJV."*

Universities, Colleges, Schools, Corporations, Churches, Quantity Buyers:
Discounts on this book are available for bulk purchases. Please contact:

SCHERF, Inc.
P.O. Box 80180
Las Vegas, NV 89180-0180
U.S.A.

Telephone (702) 243-4895 • FAX (702) 243-7460

This book is dedicated to my beloved children Alexander, Deborah, Daniel and David. May this book point them and every reader in the right direction to find and obtain objective truth, so that they will never have to suffer the vicious and devastating effects of depression.

He sent His word,
and healed them,
and delivered them
from their destructions.

PSALM 107:20

CONTENTS

INTRODUCTION   13

1   **IDENTITY CRISIS**
SELF-ANALYSIS   19
The Search • 20
Wanna be Loved? • 21
The Destroyed Image of an Idol • 23
Appreciating the Work of a Celebrity • 27
Wrong Sources for Deriving an Identity • 28
Subjectivity vs. Objectivity • 35
Life-Changing Decisions • 36
Depression Must be Defined • 37
Positive Thinking and Objective Truth • 41
Cause and Effect of Depression • 42
Trying to Change The Unchangeable • 45
Some Thoughts • 50

2   **LOVING YOURSELF**   51
Don't Dwell on Negative Things • 51
What Do You Like About Yourself? • 56
Accepting Your Imperfections • 59
Making Time for Yourself • 66

3 **LOVE, SEX AND MARRIAGE** 75
Definition of Love • 75
Marriage and Infidelity • 79
Homosexuality • 85
Sexual Encounters • 87

4 **OBJECTIVE TRUTH** 97
Objective Truth Defined • 97
How Does Objective Truth Work? • 98
The Authority of Objective Truth • 100
Objective Truth in Action • 102
Discovering Objective Truth • 104
Accepting Objective Truth • 111

5 **MORE THAN CONQUERORS** 117
Healing of the Soul • 119
Conquer the Impossible • 126

6 **A PERFECT LIFE
ABUNDANT LIFE** 133
True Identity • 136
Never Alone Again • 141
Clear Thinking • Correct Focus • 145
Abundant Life • 150

7 ABSOLUTE DELIVERANCE, FREEDOM AND VICTORY   153

Deliverance • 155
Freedom • 160
Victory • 162

8 THE SUPERNATURAL REALITY   167

Hell • 168
Satan • 173
Psychics • UFOs and Aliens • 180
Angels • 185
Luck • 186

9 ULTIMATE PROSPERITY   191

Blessings and Prosperity • 192
Purpose and Genuine Happiness • 202

ABOUT THE AUTHOR   213

ACKNOWLEDGMENTS   215

RECOMMENDED READINGS   217

MEET WITH DIETMAR SCHERF IN PERSON   218

**OTHER BOOKS BY
DIETMAR SCHERF**   *219*

RELAXED MUSIC   *220*

SPREADING THE NEWS   *221*

ORGANIZING SCHERF MEETINGS   *222*

ORDER FORM   *223*

INTRODUCTION

There is no doubt about the fact that depression is truly a killer in the literal sense of the word. Depression is not a respecter of persons. It attacks every age group from teenagers to the elderly, and it surfaces in every social class from the poor to the super rich. Depression attacks men and women alike. Because of an environment where depression is prevalent, even young children suffer from depression to some degree or at least from the effects of depression from those people around them that suffer from depression. National borders cannot stop depression from entering and it is present in every nation around the globe. It's a vicious and deceitful spirit creeping in through all kinds of avenues trying to destroy mankind. Depression is affecting all of us in one way or the other.

While self-destruction in whatever form always accompanies depression, suicide is the ultimate result of self-destruction. Today, the seemingly last resort, namely suicide, prevails not only as a thought with many depression victims, but the actual suicide rate is rapidly on the increase. Because of the accessibility of news on radio, television and the Internet, and the images portrayed in movies, and because of bad examples of so called suicide doctors that promote suicide as a seemingly normal last resort, we have become desensitized towards the selfish and tragic act of suicide. This makes depression a very dangerous illness and mental condition. Because depression is indeed infectious, we're all at risk.

Considering everything, this book has been in the making for virtually over two decades. When I was a teenager I became extremely depressed and finally manic depression developed in my own life. At the age of twelve I was already sobbing for hours, because of being severely depressed. For many years I had to battle various forms of depression, resulting often in suicidal thoughts and occasionally leading to suicidal behavior. After having seen so much pain and tragic outcomes from depression, this book was a must for me to write. I'm also aware of the only real cure and only solution to avoid and overcome depression on a permanent basis effectively, which is the only thing that has ever really worked in my life and in the lives of thousands of people. I think this book can be very helpful to every human being no matter what their current state of mind might be.

After thinking for over a year about how we could communicate this subject in the form of a book most effectively, including and offering proper analyses and precise solutions, we were able to produce in this book a unique blend of a psychological and spiritual approach. This type of approach is very rare and hard to find in any book pertaining to this topic.

There is complete healing available from depression. It can be done without medication and it really doesn't take much effort on your part to receive absolute deliverance from depression. In this book we'll show you how you can overcome depression if you're currently suffering from it. But we also explain how you can avoid situations and tendencies that may lead to depressive moods. We go even further in that we reveal to you how easy it is to develop proper self-esteem and to maintain it through every circumstance of life whatsoever. We'll also show you how you can obtain a victorious life with true joy, substance and purpose.

In order to learn how to avoid and overcome depression, we won't go on a head trip, but instead we'll go through the simple, but very effective step of how this seemingly impossible task is accomplished in reality. In fact, this procedure shouldn't be difficult, but instead it should be a positive and enjoyable experience. Even if you have seemingly no problem with depression at this moment in your life, it certainly can't hurt to take preventive measures now so that the downbeat cycles of depression won't be able to creep in and attack you out of the blue some day in the future. Ultimately, of course, it's going to be your own decision to accept the cure, solution and the preventive measures offered and provided in this book.

We have to realize that we live in a world in which negatives are emphasized. Not that it truly is a world of negatives, but because for certain reasons which we'll also explain a little bit in this book, negative things just seem to dominate our lives. If you don't believe it just turn on your "holy shrine"—the television—and watch the news. Or simply scan the headlines of a newspaper or news magazine. Compare how many murders, crimes, accidents and other sad happenings are reported in comparison to the combined positive news mentioned. You'll be shocked. If you don't watch the standard news channels go to your favorite gossip column or show and count the negative stories versus the positive anecdotes.

We're influenced by negatives on a consistent basis. Negatives are emphasized and exalted way above any positive aspect, and that's a big dilemma which we all encounter. This book will explain vital solutions applicable to every person individually to change their own life in this regard for the better, and in turn produce positive effects in their world around them, without being caught up and ensnared in a frustrating self-help program. Everybody who takes the contents of this book seriously will not only derive plenty of benefits for themselves almost instantly, but will produce a positive environment around them automatically. It is my desire that as many people as possible around the world will hear the message contained in this book—it not only will change their lives, but may secure their eternal destiny, too.

You'll learn the lost art of loving yourself properly. In my experience people are almost always embarrassed when this subject is considered in a private conversation or a seminar. This reveals to me that people have a misconception of loving themselves and that they simply don't know how to love themselves properly. It is very important to love yourself. We'll show you how it's done properly and how it works and what difference it will make in your life.

It is only then when I love myself that I'll be able to truly love others. Loving others then won't be much of an effort, but instead has much more to do with your mind—with the thoughts that you think towards other people resulting in healthy emotions no matter how they treat you. The same is true with loving yourself, it's not really a self-effort to love yourself, but rather a mindset—certain thoughts that you think will produce healthy emotions appreciating your healthy state of mind. Many associate loving yourself with egotism when in fact it is the opposite.

In our society, seemingly everybody lives for themselves. "We're living in a competitive society," many will say, "and therefore we've got to look out for our own interest." Yeah? Is it so? What are your goals in life? Have you arrived yet? What do you know about yourself? Who are you? What is this life all about? Do you feel hurt, bitter, insecure, lonely, stressed out or even burned out? Are you quite successful, is your career advancing and are you making more money than ever, but does it still seem like that something is lacking or missing and that you're not getting anywhere? Are you discouraged because your longtime "best friends" all of a sudden have betrayed you and stabbed you in the back? Do you feel that your life doesn't amount to much? Do you really love someone? Do you feel loved? How about your self-esteem? Can you look into the mirror and say honestly from the bottom of your heart "I love me" and really, really mean it? Are you able to do this?

Lots of questions; and this list of questions could be continued on an on. It's my prayer that this book will enrich your life and provide answers to your most important questions that you've asked yourself for some time now. It's my hope (hope = confident expectation) that the message contained in this book will come across to you understandably for easy practical application to really provide unique insight and true help in time of need for every reader. Please enjoy!

Yours truly,

Dietmar Scherf

Las Vegas, Nevada
December 1997

1

IDENTITY CRISIS
SELF-ANALYSIS

Throughout every culture in history an identity crisis has almost always resulted in a major tragedy when it occurred. An identity crisis can occur on a national level and also within a corporation or organization. But inevitably sooner or later each person will face an identity crisis in their own personal life. We'll deal with the identity crisis on a personal level, because established and qualified leaders that have dealt with their own personal identity crisis, will eventually be able to take care of any national, corporate or organizational identity crisis through their leadership.

THE SEARCH

Walking through life we're on a continuous search trying to figure out various things about ourselves — things that bother us, e.g. Who are we? Does our life really count? Are we being truly loved by someone? This includes the search for answers to a series of questions like: Where are we coming from? Where are we going? What is the purpose of life? Is there life after death? Or, when tragedy strikes, "Why me?"

Life is made up of choices. To temporarily satisfy our search for unanswered questions, which often is the ground for internal conflict, we accept certain superficial answers and images as temporary solutions. But these answers are only temporary, superficial and are in fact pseudo-answers without any substance and are lacking the foundation of objective truth.

When we were small kids we probably looked up to our parents as role models, to mommy and daddy, if we've been blessed to have been raised in a home with two parents. As family values deteriorate it becomes much harder to find a home with the traditional environment. Instead of having mommy and daddy as their role models, even small children are being manipulated to look up to fictitious "heroes" promoted on television and in print media. Seeds of a future identity crisis are being sown into those little ones at an average age of five years. As adults we're standing by watching it happen in front of our eyes doing nothing, and may even support this terrible influence on our children in one way or the other, without realizing it.

When we ourselves became teenagers this search became very obvious as we may have looked up to certain celebrities as idols to derive some sort of temporary identity from them. These idols can be found in the world of entertainment, sports, politics, art, business and perhaps even in religion. Often teenagers will lean to music and sport figures to satisfy their urge for a derived identity. This derived pseudo-identity becomes obvious in the way we dress, talk and behave. Putting posters on the wall at home may reflect these tendencies outwardly to some degree. True, we all need something or someone to look up to. Role models, leaders— someone that we can identify with in the desperate attempt of being accepted, or bluntly put: the hope of being loved unconditionally.

WANNA BE LOVED?

When Madonna (the singer and motion picture star) gave birth to her first baby she said in an interview that now she'll have an opportunity to give unconditional love to a human being. Dennis Rodman (the basketball player) said pretty much the same thing when he admitted in an interview that he just has a need to be loved and that he wants to be loved unconditionally. In fact, there is nothing wrong with this desire. As human beings we have a certain emotional frame and are beings that want to love and are in need to be loved. If possible we would like to be loved unconditionally. Meaning, we just want to be loved without expectations of returning anything for being loved the way we are—without having demands put on ourselves for changing ourselves. We're in need of unconditional love.

No, we don't want to change, but we simply want to be loved just the way we are—unconditionally. That's our innermost desire. In search to fulfill this desire we do a lot of different things just to find out later in life that nothing really worked. Sometimes it seems that this or that works for a little while, but still something is missing.

Do you think that Princess Diana was happy and free of depression? Well, think again, because throughout her public life she reflected in appearances and interviews that she suffered severely from depression. She had an eating disorder and felt rejected. While it may have seemed that things were getting better during the last year of her life, she immersed herself into philanthropic causes. And of course, it's great to pursue such a noble endeavor, but it is an absolute requirement that a person involved in such efforts is getting their inner being at least basically in order before going out publicly on a broad scale to love others. Why? You must learn to love yourself, which also means that you have to accept yourself unconditionally just the way you are. You have to define certain things in your soul first in order to enjoy the freedom that comes from knowing these certain things about yourself. This is also for your protection so that when you go out there you won't become a burnout. Doing good unto people doesn't necessarily mean that everything is going to be hunky-dory from now on. Every person that does good will face opposition and it's easy to get hurt. Therefore proper self-esteem must be developed and certain crucial details about life and yourself must be learned and understood in the course of preparation for such a task. Otherwise a battle with severe depression is inevitable and it's easy to become a burnout.

THE DESTROYED IMAGE OF AN IDOL

Do you think that lots of money, success, fame, relentless pleasures and seeming significance in society can provide unconditional love and happiness? Think again and look at the lives of the many movie and music stars. Check out the biographies of the wealthiest people in the world. Once again you'll be in for a shock, if you think that fame, things, money, etc. can "buy" you love and happiness.

Often the personal lives of celebrities are shattered and this is reflected by a series of divorces, infidelities, drug abuse, etc. Look at the life of singer Elton John who had big money and tremendous success already at the age of thirty. He was a victim of depression for most of his life and nearly killed himself several times through attempted suicides. By the way, Elton John isn't a rare example. The more we study the lives of celebrities the more we find out about their loneliness and their desperate attempts to satisfy their innermost desires leaving them discouraged and severely depressed in the end. Often this may not be very obvious. Many motion picture stars and music celebrities pretend to have a very outgoing personality. They may be able to make a strong impression and hide their real self and desperate needs for some time. But more often than not their projected self-image is merely a façade destined to crumble sooner or later.

The singer Boy George from England confirmed this fact in a recent interview. He battled a heroin habit for years and felt lonely, depressed and went from one identity crisis into the other trying to find his own identity. Imagine the thousands of fans that were seeking to derive some sort of identity from Boy George for themselves, when he himself seemingly didn't have one and was constantly in an identity crisis. British rock singer David Bowie had similar problems in the seventies and consistently struggled to find his own real identity, reinventing himself with pseudo-identities over and over again.

Another example is Rob Pilatus from the former duo Milli Vanilli. They were financially poor and through some odd circumstances they became highly visible celebrities in the late eighties. All they wanted was to make some money and meet a lot of girls. Their wish came true and they became very wealthy and famous celebrating their success with lots of women. But one day the pseudo-world and dream of Milli Vanilli collapsed just as quickly as it was built. Turning to drugs to solve his inner conflicts, Rob Pilatus went many times through rehab and became manic depressive. Bitterness and anger were stored up in his soul and finally he thought suicide would be the only possible answer. He survived the suicide attempt. Wealth, fame, pleasures and the fulfillment of all your dreams can't buy honest acceptance by true friends, nor can it provide pure unconditional love. All this surely can't provide a real substantial identity either.

There is nothing heroic about rebels either. Teenagers often have a tendency to rebel and to follow their idols. But often those idols struggle themselves with who they really are and are decadent, depressed and in many cases commit suicide. Suicide may happen willfully or through a negligent and careless act or lifestyle, for instance through a drug overdose, etc. Sid Vicious (member of the former British punk-rock band "Sex Pistols") was one of the ultimate rebel embodiments in the late seventies before he killed himself in a room of an infamous hotel in New York.

Lots of people with success, money and fame have wretched lives. Why are we discussing this? Simply, because as mentioned before, even in our teenage years we begin to look up to certain people that seemingly "have made it." Often we try to model our thinking, our ideas, our value system and, if possible, even our lifestyle after these so-called role models. Or should we say idols? We love their movies, music and lifestyle, and certainly these things will influence our thinking and behavior in various ways. We want to become like them, or at least take on some part of them. Remember when you were a teenager listening to the music and watching the movies becoming infatuated with those performers? It wasn't just for entertainment sake, it was to find, or rather derive, an identity from them for yourself. Maybe some little part would rub off.

Maybe you grew up in a working-class family and those idols were larger than life. There was this glimpse of hope for success, of changing a mundane boring everyday life. But in all this we forgot to look behind the scenes and were blinded by the glamour of the stage. For a performer the actual time of stage performances in front of an audience is usually only for a couple of hours a day. Even if a few hours of practice are added to this schedule, each performer will find quite some time available to them to be spent off stage. Away from the limelight each performer is basically trying to live a normal life. The routine of life is not removed from them and they must deal with it one way or the other. They're busy trying to fulfill their desires and making their dreams come true—just like everybody else.

Therefore using a movie star, or a rock star, or a sports figure as an idol or image to derive an identity from for yourself is absolutely insane. The fact is that doing so eventually must lead to an identity crisis, because our "role models" are having an identity crisis themselves. Check out the lives of popular idols such as James Dean, Elvis Presley, Janis Joplin, etc. who all suffered from severe depressions throughout most of their lives and died early. No matter if you like their movies or music, the real issue is their personal life and honestly these people did not live very desirable personal lives.

APPRECIATING THE WORK OF A CELEBRITY

There is nothing wrong with appreciating the work and accomplishments of a celebrity. I like certain movies and certain records, certain paintings, certain sports, certain books, etc. and I like the achievements of certain individuals in business, entertainment, sports, philanthropy, etc. While I may like a certain aspect of one or the other individual and/or his or her work and/or achievements, it most certainly doesn't mean that I let myself become infatuated with them nor do I derive my identity from them. Of course, I've done it and surely everybody else has done it to some degree at one point. But many people never let go of it and this is also why depression is so widespread. Holding on to something superficial, unreal—an illusion and a fantasy not dealing with reality is a very painful experience.

WRONG SOURCES FOR
DERIVING AN IDENTITY

When we get older most people try to derive an identity
no longer from idols, but rather from their education,
job or professional position, relationships, money and
material things.

Greed for more money and excessive materialism is
definitely a killer, too. To keep up with the Joneses and
the world system on a materialistic scale is devastating.
Trying to be "In" is stressful. In most of the countries of
the western civilized hemisphere we're living in an
environment of consumer-goods overkill. Today, the
consumer has the availability of a broad selection of
hundreds of models from a toothbrush to cars, homes,
televisions, etc. It's definitely an absolute consumer-
product overkill. Whatever is great today is junk tomorrow. Car manufacturers change their car lines every
few years. It's hard to keep up, if you're a slave to the
latest fashion or consumer trends. There are still some
products that may in fact improve our standard of living
and may even represent value to some extent. Something may save us time or money, for instance.

To derive an identity from certain products that you
own and show off is ludicrous. I like the example of Sam
Walton (founder of Wal-Mart) who as a multibillionaire
always drove around in a pickup truck. He didn't care
about status symbols when it came to a car. For decades
he lived in the same modest house which he built before
he became super rich. Even as a multibillionaire he

didn't change his residence and he seemingly had no desire to build a luxurious mansion to show off his enormous financial wealth. Sam Walton didn't derive his identity from his cars or his home. I don't know where he derived his identity from and I don't know if he had it figured out in the end or not. He may have derived it from his mega-billion-dollar empire or something else.

Take, for instance, Bill Gates (founder of Microsoft Corporation) at age forty-one with a net worth of around $40 billion the richest man in the United States. Where does he derive his identity from or does he not have time to think about it? Billions of dollars could serve as a type of blindfold to avoid dealing with the issue and to allow a superficial unfulfilled life without ever realizing it. Still, something inside of you continues to be a cause of discomfort—an unfulfilled desire for something which you just can't define. The money helps temporarily to overlook this issue, but when sickness or personal tragedy strikes, money can't provide sufficient comfort.

People derive their identity from who they are on the job, from their position and from their achievements. When they lose their jobs their world collapses. Over the past few years we've not only seen fired postal workers go berserk killing innocent people and usually themselves, but also company executives go nuts doing a lot of harm to innocent parties and themselves.

Or are you looking for the biggest house on the block to boost your image? This whole image thing drives people crazy. There is nothing against having and owning nice automobiles, luxury homes and plenty of material possessions, or to accept the best job offer possible, but these things shouldn't become our life—each of these things are only bits and pieces to compliment our life.

When these things become our life, meaning when most of our energy, attention and concentration goes into stuff like this and we have expectations that these things will provide us with happiness, fulfillment and true purpose, etc., eventually our life will be destroyed and will seem worthless and wasted. We're being tutored from a very young age to be like that. Who has the nicest bicycle? Who has the most toys? Who wears brand-name shoes, shirts and jeans? As we grow older these images continue to be fed into our minds by TV commercials, ads, song lyrics, movies and articles in lifestyle magazines. For the purpose of a reality check simply ask yourself if there is anything or any product or job in your life that you couldn't let go of without becoming deeply depressed. Are you content with your life? Can you lean back in a rocking chair taking a deep breath of fresh air enjoying and treasuring it as the greatest thing in life?

For ladies at first it was a nice dress advancing to a complete wardrobe of so many clothes that you'd never be able to wear them even if you'd live to be over a hundreds years old, adding consistently new things. Years go by as girls are desperately looking for the right guy. Being disappointed along the way in the search for some sort of identity.

For guys it's a stereo, and from a nice used car things advance to the burning desire of owning a fancy new car, and then on to an apartment and finally to a house. In between maybe getting married to the prettiest girl around. Then the search goes on into exciting and thrilling new hobbies, desperately trying to fill this undefined void inside, trying to find an identity that could be potentially comfortable to live with. It's a search for a self-image with a measure of prestige that would provide acceptance and appreciation from the so called friends and within the community. More and more things are needed to keep up. In the process, of course, many things happen and it's like a race—but it's a rat race. Children come along and the race begins again with a new generation.

A lady, who was married for a few years, once called in for counseling, and said that her husband was working day and night to save enough money to purchase a certain used automobile. For months his conversations centered around getting this used car. Their marriage suffered from his preoccupation of getting this old car. After many months of agony he finally got the car, but his wife had a nervous breakdown and was admitted to a mental institution. Certainly, the car wasn't the only reason for her to have this nervous breakdown, but part of it was surely the tremendous attention her husband put on getting this old car while being insensitive to the needs of his wife and neglecting her completely. Part of the excitement was the expectation period until getting the car and he got all worked up emotionally. Once he had the car sitting in his driveway the excitement fizzled out just a couple of weeks later. He also realized that the car couldn't boost his self-image intrinsically which he was hoping for.

This happens over and over again as one spouse puts all his attention and energy on and into something while neglecting the other partner. It might be a job or career, a thing (e.g. a car, house, etc.), a desire for a baby, or whatever. We always think that this thing or that thing will be able to provide us with the happiness that we are longing for. Once such a thing is obtained we quickly find out that this certain thing couldn't meet our expectations. Then we find another thing and the cycle starts all over again. Life goes on and precious time is wasted on our selfish pursuits of happiness..

Another example and a true story of the devastating effects of the rat race was the gentleman who worked very hard for many years to buy himself a brand new Mercedes Benz. He was very excited when he finally received his car. But just a few months later, when he was parking his beloved Benz in the parking lot of a shopping center, a small scratch on the side of the car set him off, causing a manic depressive reaction resulting in suicide. He killed himself for a scratch on a car that could have been repaired for a hundred bucks or so. Thought projections shot through his mind dictating to his brain impulses that his world had just crumbled and that he lost everything, when in fact nothing really serious has happened.

There will always be a better and bigger house, a

nicer car, and the potential of making more money. There will always be people that are more beautiful then we are. If we're not aware of the remedy for depression, and when sooner or later the realization kicks in that it's impossible to keep up with the status quo and to make it, even when you seemingly have made it, it opens the door for depression. Money and things can't buy your way out of it. Somebody once said that the devil can wall us in, but he can't roof us in, therefore there is always a way of escape. Living by a temporal value system, of course, will never let us see or provide us with the hope of such an emergency exit.

When ladies get married they almost always expect their husbands to be Superman. As time goes by and reality sets in, the Superman image is all of a sudden gone. Meaning, Superman cannot provide the desired ultra identity of strength and invincibility a wife once saw in her husband. Ultimately, in search of security and in fact for some sort of identity the question of the existence of greener pastures will arise. There are no greener pastures, but based on today's divorce rate seemingly not too many people believe this fact and want to find out for themselves.

Bottom line, a spouse cannot provide a true identity for you, but he or she can certainly be of help to you to develop proper self-esteem, if he or she is right on in this regard. It is always sad to see the world of an individual utterly destroyed over the death of a spouse. Sometimes for years they mourn the loss of their mate, wasting their life entering into severe depression. Don't misunderstand, there is certainly a time of mourning for the loss of a spouse. But after this certain time of mourning, life must go on for the surviving mate. Later in this chapter we discuss the devastating effects of trying to change the unchangeable.

There are many things that offer themselves as a source of identity, but almost all sources aside from objective truth will lead to depression sooner or later in one way or the other. Depression is destructive not only to the victimized person itself, but often to the loved ones around them, because they suffer from it, too. We know of cases where the mother or the father was so depressed that in his suicide rage he also killed his children and spouse. While such tragic scenarios may not affect us immediately, we must be aware that depression can lead to such horrible actions, and it could hit home unexpectedly and spontaneously. It's possible. With all the violent movies and images of violence displayed in front of our eyes on a day to day basis, these violent acts are stored up in our memory systems as a point of reference, even though in most cases only as a last resort. But we've become desensitized towards violence and death, and we're virtually indoctrinated by seeing it all the time, and we're no longer shocked by a reported suicide or murder. An intensification of cir-cumstances or an accumulation of certain circumstances could trigger distinctive thought processes leading to devastating actions, and every person could potentially snap in a second, if no preventive guards have been established.

SUBJECTIVITY VS. OBJECTIVITY

At a very young age we were trained to become subjective and therefore temporarily lost the ability to become individuals with true objectivity. Subjectivity leads to emotionalism in a bad sense. There is nothing wrong with healthy emotions and the expression of such healthy emotions, but a highly emotional person is a trip destined to make major mistakes in life. We're all human beings and we have emotions (emotions = mental and/or physical responses or reactions to causes, situations, circumstances, etc.). Rarely do we ever learn to develop our emotions properly. Yes, we're taught to behave a certain way in society when certain things happen, because of the manifestations and effects certain emotional outbursts may have on others and ourselves. Regarding the details of life and various circumstances, we simply do not receive the proper training for our emotional response systems.

In road traffic you can see a variety of uncontrolled emotional outbursts. Healthy emotions are very beneficial for yourself and the world around you. The emotions are a part of the soul. (The soul is made up of five parts and consists of the conscience, self-consciousness, the emotions, the free will or volition, and the intellect or mind).

In order to acquire a proper self-image and identity we must derive it from an objective source. Otherwise, without exception, we're doomed to extract a useless, self-destructive, and dangerous pseudo-identity always

leading us sooner or later—because of internal empti-
ness—into depression. To obtain a false identity is very
dangerous, because little by little our chemical balance
is altered and becomes disturbed. That's why many
people suffering from depression take medication trying to correct their degenerate chemical balance. But,
medication can only serve as a temporary solution,
relief or provision for a very short period of time and is
unable to cure the root of the problem permanently.

LIFE-CHANGING DECISIONS

Life is made up of choices. Down the road we've made a
series of choices. Changes usually occur gradually,
meaning one step at a time. Most humans avoid dramatic radical changes, because they're afraid of making
radical decisions. Making such radical decisions also
means that one old familiar thing comes to an end while
we enter into or take on an unexplored new thing. Once
a radical decision regarding a radical change has been
made, it often makes it impossible to return to the
familiar old and this keeps people from making radical
decisions. This is one reason why lots of people continue
year after year in their familiar same old misery, and
are seemingly unable to do anything about it. As human
beings we're afraid of the unfamiliar new thing.

The older we get the more difficult it will be to allow
radical changes in our life, because we don't want to go

through the hassle of exploring the unfamiliar new thing. It is sad to see people grow older and to give up on the refreshing juice of life. They are often disappointed with certain aspects of their lives and are actually bitter inside. They feel betrayed and have retired to their own little world which they hope will serve as a hideaway, but in fact has become a prison. In search for an identity throughout their lives they finally found out that the certain idol they adored for decades just couldn't provide the identity they were looking for. Jobs, relationships, money and material possessions couldn't provide a true lasting identity, so in the end they don't have a true individual identity. They'll sometimes accept a standardized, but distorted senior-citizen image for an identity, which can be very depressing, too, because it's once again just another pseudo-identity.

DEPRESSION MUST BE DEFINED

In order to deal with depression effectively it must be defined. One definition for depression can be understood as being unable to get what you want within a desired time frame. Your desires may be derived from images that you have perceived at one point in your life and which are replayed over and over again in your mind. During this process your imagination goes wild with ideas about the images of your idols and so-called role models you've encountered during your life. Realizing the disability to fulfill your desires will create frustration within, expressing itself initially with the subjective feeling of being inadequate, being a loser or having lost—in some cases—everything (especially when depression enters into the manic state).

A manic-depressive person experiences an advanced state of depression. While the initial cycle of depression may go on over a stretch of years or once in a year, continuously intensifying, in its advanced manic form a person may experience the up-and-down cycles dozens of times a day. There will be feelings of undefined sadness, they will feel rejected, worthless without any hope of betterment, even though an emotional upswing will happen through some thought or incident at a bottom of the down cycle, propelling this individual back up again into stratospheric heights emotionally. But this up and down and up and down is the "killer." It's an emotional roller coaster which drives a person crazy.

Examples: A millionaire wakes up happy, but in need of a pencil suddenly is unable to locate a pencil and in his mind he really thinks he lost all his money and all his possessions—his mind signals to the emotions that his world has just been destroyed when in reality nothing devastating has happened. A husband leaves the house for work in the morning and being in a hurry he doesn't kiss his wife good-bye, and thoughts enter her mind that he may have a girlfriend—and it burns a hole into her soul even though it's not true—it's only in the mind. At the workplace you did a tremendous job, but nobody recognizes it with a word of appreciation or similar gesture, and thoughts will enter your mind that you'll be fired soon and that nobody cares and eventually that your great job wasn't that great after all. It creates tremendous anxiety. Princess Diana said in an interview that when she got married she really tried so very hard to do everything right to fit her role as the Princess of Wales, etc., but that nobody ever complimented her on her efforts and not even regarding the obvious accomplishments she obtained. With the proper self-esteem it wouldn't matter if anybody acknowledges what we're doing, even though it feels really good to receive encouragement and appreciation.

To further define depression it is accepting lies and negativity from vague mind projections as being reality, when in fact these projections are not true at all, but are only vain imaginations and projections without substance and truth. Negative communication and negative incidents produce mind projections and vain imaginations. The mind has the ability to exaggerate things. The more we talk about negative things the more these things will be exaggerated and intensified. When we dwell on such lies long enough lines are being formed and are being carved into our memory systems. The more often we ponder and meditate the same lies and negative thoughts the more "real" the illusion will become and it will affect our nervous systems and chemical balances, and will alter our states of mind and chemical balances gradually. Imagine living in an illusion and accepting it as reality? This means that down the road our response systems will malfunction and instead of objective responses we'll react to every little thing. Sad, isn't it?

Depression is in fact a supernatural phenomena and therefore it doesn't make much sense trying to treat depression with a natural approach.

Relax, don't freak out—at this early point of the book we're still analyzing the situation, and we must define certain details, so that it is easier for us to understand the whole process of how depressions are formed and come about, and what depressions are and that depression must be dealt with head on. Your case is not hopeless, nor is any other case hopeless. Don't forget the subtitles of this book "Avoiding & Overcoming Depression • Developing Proper Self-Esteem • Obtaining a Victorious Life with Joy, Substance and Purpose" which are also meant to be promises, and we'll get to it shortly and explain it in detail.

Nobody is immune to the onslaught of depressive moods and cycles, but there are preventive measures we can take to neutralize and eliminate such potential attacks and even avoid depression effectively.

POSITIVE THINKING
AND OBJECTIVE TRUTH

Here are some thoughts regarding the power of positive thinking. Genuine optimistic thinking can be very beneficial when it isn't done in subjectivity, but instead is based on objective truth. Yes, positive thinking is powerful and can be very helpful, but the positive thoughts must be derived from objective truth regarding all kinds of subjects and issues about yourself, life and God. Otherwise you would end up once again with a structure of lies, even though such thoughts seem to be positive in the beginning, but eventually these "positive" lies will lead into depression. To be an optimist based on objective truth is healthy. To rely on positive thinking based on subjectivity may seem to work temporarily, but is ultimately just as devastating as negativity. We can't get around it—we need to find objective truth and then we need to apply objective truth in every aspect of our life, which is simply a decision-making process.

Loaded with objective truth we'll be able to acquire a true and genuine identity, because definition and answers will be provided to most of our essential questions regarding life, etc. Often as a last resort, people adhere to religion and enter into a religious program. It won't work. Usually an abstract god image is mixed into such philosophies. No matter what religion it may be, an abstract god image is just another type of an idol and any identity obtained from an abstract god image will eventually also lead to severe depression. Of course, there is the true God as explained and revealed in the Word of God. And while we may not comprehend much about the true God, the Bible clearly defines and explains everything we need to know about the true God.

It is essential to consult objective truth regarding every aspect of life. Objective truth has a qualified answer to virtually all our key questions. Objective truth knows everything and is able to provide us with the necessary faith to believe its definitions and to empower us for practical application with its accurate guidance.

CAUSE AND EFFECT OF DEPRESSION

To acquire a proper identity and self-image I must know who I am and I must receive answers to essential questions regarding my existence and purpose in life. Otherwise depression will always creep in with the intention to destroy me. Depression is a supernatural spirit of destruction. Once a person has become a victim of depression this individual has been infected by this vicious spirit and it must be dealt with head on. Otherwise it will continue to grow and destroy not only the victimized person, but will also infect other individuals.

While depression starts in the mind and in the process destroys every part of the soul, it will also affect the nervous system and the chemical balance will be ruined.

At this point we must mention that some depressions are caused by drugs prescribed within distinctive medical treatments, e.g. regarding pain treatments, etc. in the case of various cancers, etc. In this book we're not specifically dealing with this type of depressions caused by the manipulation of chemical balances during such medical treatments as just mentioned. The cause of these depressions is obviously from outside influences and from effects of chemical substances prescribed during such treatments. These drugs will alter the normal chemical balances and trigger depressions simply because of a physiological fact of chemical imbalance. That's why sometimes natural pain treatments based on a herbal formula are better, because the normal chemical balance will usually not be significantly altered with natural formulas. But these natural treatments are normally not scientifically proven methods and therefore are not widely accepted by professionals in modern medicine. They may also not be effective in the case of every individual.

Often the physical expressions of various illnesses including malignant tumors and ulcers are the final result of severe depressions. How can this be? As we have impressions and take various feelings, facts, philosophies, etc. into us we also have the need to express ourselves. Stress and anxiety are also a cause, form or result of depression. We may cry, scream, or perform irrational activities. Remember depression directly affects our emotions. Depression may produce feelings of anger, bitterness, anxiety, a continuous pessimistic and hopeless outlook of life, the loss of self-respect, unworthiness, undefined and unexplained sadness, stress and rejection. If a person becomes introverted the internal vent so to speak is shut off and instead of expressing feelings, etc. everything is accumulated inside. This cannot go on for very long. It's like a heating system: eventually the heat must be released somehow, or the oven, stove, etc. will explode because of the intensified energy accumulated within. So if there is no release of such energy, the body will take on this task by itself and will release it through physical discomfort and eventually through illnesses and the production of malignant tumors, ulcers or cancer throughout the body, which once again is self-destructive. At this point let us mention that cancer can be produced through a variety of other things. Depression is just one of many aspects and causes that can lead to such physical illnesses.

To illustrate please consider a balloon. You put air into the balloon and when it reaches a certain size it is a fun object to play with and it has a purpose. Even if you let the air out of the balloon and let go of the balloon it still is fun as the balloon roars through the air. But if you put too much air into the balloon the potential experience of fun and entertainment will immediately vanish and all of a sudden the balloon becomes a dangerous object. The balloon will explode and therefore will be destroyed and rendered useless. During the explosion process parts of the exploded balloon could potentially hurt the person boosting the air into the balloon and also bystanders.

What goes in must come out. What goes up must come down. Natural principles that are relevant throughout most components of life.

TRYING TO CHANGE
THE UNCHANGEABLE

Trying to change the unchangeable will also lead to depression. The unchangeable cannot be changed. Example: Millions of people always discuss how if they would have done this and that differently in the past, things would have turned out another way, usually for the better they suppose. This, of course, is pure speculation and in most cases nobody can know what might have been if this or that would have been done or said differently. The past cannot be changed—it already happened and it is gone. We can certainly learn from past experiences and enjoy the fragrance of memory. But every second of our life is a brand new experience. And every second once occurred in the present is at that very moment immediately gone and becomes part of the past, which then in turn becomes unchangeable as it has already happened and won't come back again.

Some individuals within my own family remain reluctant to let go of the past. They always speculate that better things would have come about if they would have done certain things differently in the past. This is all pure speculation. It's an absolute fact that things in the past haven't been done differently, but have happened exactly the way the record books of history have recorded it—just the way things have actually happened and were done in the past. These things cannot be changed. Trying to change the unchangeable is a frustrating experience and creates a lot of unnecessary and even painful anxiety leading eventually to massive depression.

Example: We all agree that the fatal accident of Princess Diana was a tragic event. After the accident the blame game began and went around. The "What if?" questions were fired through the air from all directions. One speculation after the other. Blaming this circumstance and pointing the finger at this group of people or at that person, etc. The blame game and the speculations could go on forever. Even a small number of facts surrounding the accident are distinctive indications and the basis of the actual events.

Let's analyze it just for a moment: Princess Diana was a public figure. A public figure is someone who is making an impression upon the public as discussed earlier in this book. This could be any kind of celebrity in the entertainment business, politics, sports, art, business, etc. These individuals are role models and seemingly epitomize something the general public or certain groups of humanity are searching for or are interested in. The media reinforces this public interest to broaden the desired impact. As individuals we're responsible for our own actions and it's our own choice to do certain things. If a public figure is very interesting because of what they represent, do, say and achieve, there is an enhanced desire by the general public to know more about this person. As also discussed earlier in this chapter, because of our desires and dreams we want to become to at least some extent just like that particular idol in the hope to derive some identity for ourselves from such a person.

Therefore, if someone is a public figure the media will report to the general public the things they do, so that the desire of the public to know more about such a celebrity is satisfied. Consequently, the private life of such a celebrity will become a very public one and photographers will be around that person most of the time. But it's still the choice of each individual to become a public figure. If someone doesn't want to be a public figure then they shouldn't plan and do things to become a celebrity. While the paparazzi may be annoying, they're just another part of the media system and the celebrity package. We must also realize that celebrities frequently use and cooperate with the media to bring attention to and promote a variety of charitable causes, etc. Usually only celebrities can interest the media in reporting about such causes and events, and therefore there is certainly a close liaison between celebrities and the media.

If a person decides to become a surgeon instead there are other things that are annoying and uncomfortable that come with this specific job. As a waitress there are again various other things that are very annoying, but a waitress has to live with it, because these certain uncomfortable aspects are a part of the package. The advice to everyone would be to go for the package that suits them seemingly best, whatever it might be, but it is also very evident that there won't be a perfect package.

Now the crucial known facts of the accident. Driving over 120mph on a city street in any city in the world is absolutely crazy. So far, my highest speed I've driven in a solid-built German automobile was 156mph on an Autobahn in Europe and I don't think I'll ever have this experience again. In city driving in Europe I once saw our car speed at just about 100mph and it was scary—and I certainly have no plans to repeat this escapade. Doing over 120mph on city streets—as is a known fact regarding the speed of the car in which Princess Diana was chauffeured in at the time of the accident—going through an underpass, was unquestionably and absolutely irresponsible, no matter what the circumstances might have been. Another fact are the results of the blood tests on the driver of the car as reported by French police indicating that the driver was seemingly under the influence of alcohol in excess of the legal limit allowed in France. Based on the facts that we all know about the influence of alcohol, even a small quantity of alcohol can inhibit your driving ability substantially. It is not a secret that any amount of alcohol or drugs will inhibit your driving ability dramatically. Driving under the influence of alcohol will create life-threatening situations for yourself and endanger everybody else on the road.

Just looking at a few basic facts of this tragic accident we can learn many things to possibly prevent similar tragedies in the future. First of all, the accident has happened and is history—and history cannot be changed, no matter how many "What if?" questions are uttered. Secondly, it's a fact that celebrities are pursued by paparazzi and if someone doesn't want to be pursued by them, then they shouldn't strive to become a celebrity—it's the free choice of every individual. Trying to outrun the paparazzi is also a choice and definitely creates potentially dangerous situations for the group of people involved and also for innocent third parties. Driving fast in city traffic or anywhere else is dangerous and consequently could result in fatalities. Remember, the legal speed limit posted is the maximum speed permitted by law, but speed limits do not guarantee your safety at these maximum speeds. This tragedy reminded us once again of the fact that alcohol and driving simply don't mix and must be avoided at all times. Laws of physics are always applicable. No matter who and what we are, these laws cannot be changed and are usually in place to set distinctive boundaries for mankind and are normally there to protect us.

SOME THOUGHTS

Learn from past experiences without becoming prejudice or subjective, and enjoy the fragrance of memory.
Dream about the future, but live in the present, because
it may determine the course of your future to at least
some extent.

Our dreams may not have limitations in our imagination, but a person consumed by making all their
dreams come true to the fullest extent will put limitations upon their experiences in the present.

We are in desperate need of sound minds—an objective system of categorical thoughts that can be accepted
by the free volition of each individual. This system has
to work automatically in every category of our lives and
throughout all life situations.

Only objective truth will provide us with true facts
about ourselves and reveal our true identity. Only
objective truth has substance and power to protect a
human soul effectively and create growth within.

We don't need to live up to the standards of others,
but we need to discover our own self-worth without the
aid of accumulating material possessions and other
outward things from a temporal value system. Objective truth will produce proper self-esteem in us display-
ing it from the inside out. Then a true personality and
identity with substance and essence is formed within us
leaving no room for depression to enter.

2

LOVING YOURSELF

In this chapter we'll discuss how it is possible and so very important to fall in love with yourself. Not subjectively, but based on objective facts. It's only when we love ourselves properly that we'll be able to truly love others. That's when every relationship receives a chance for success.

DON'T DWELL ON NEGATIVE THINGS

As explained in the previous chapter it doesn't make much sense trying to analyze and ponder things that happened in the past. Thinking about what you or they could have said or done differently will eat you up.

Modern psychology often suggests that you relive your past to find that little something that may have caused all the problems in your life. Sometimes they hypnotize you or may even plant thoughts and suggest possible scenarios, which are all subjective and based on speculation. The true cause of depression is never found by searching your past for possible answers. In fact, you will enter into blame games and often the anger is then concentrated on a parent or on the husband or wife which will cause even more distress and damages. Frequently patients enter into codependency and week after week they consult with their counselor never really solving any root problem, but receiving only momentary pseudo-relief, which is eventually even more damaging.

The unchangeable cannot be changed. The past is unchangeable. Yes, to some degree it is possible to learn from the experiences in the past and the fragrance of positive memories is certainly enjoyable. Positive experiences in the past will automatically encourage us and provide hope and an optimistic outlook. But we do not need to search the past to find a distinctive isolated incident or experience that may have traumatized us creating all our current problems. Such a search for possible answers would only distract us and eventually can't do us any good. In fact it will create only a much bigger dilemma for us while solving none of the presently existing problems.

Negative experiences in the past can really destroy us, if we consistently focus our attention on them and dwell on them month after month. Sure, there are certain negative experiences from the past which are occasionally recalled in our memory system to actually protect us. But these thoughts are just flashes. Example: If you were once robbed in a dark spot of a parking garage you'll be more cautious next time whenever you park your car in a parking garage. There are particular memories of negative experiences that will help us avoid mistakes, accidents, etc. in the present and in the future. The key to this is that instead of meditating on these negative experiences we simply need to accept these experiences and to preferably forget about them or store them away in the unconsciousness.

It is also important not to let negative experiences produce prejudice in us, which can easily happen. For instance, if a black man robbed a bank, it certainly doesn't mean that all black men are robbers, and in fact only a small percentage of this specific race may have such tendencies. If a white man once molested a child, it certainly doesn't mean that all white males are child molesters. If there is a pattern of getting hurt a lot or if we've been ripped off consistently it is very difficult and nearly impossible to trust people again and again. But we must trust others. It doesn't mean that we act stupid and relentlessly trust this person over here and that person over there, but instead we trust people by remaining in control at least to some extent. Where is this fine line? If you can't sleep well at night you may have lost control and trusted someone a little too much.

A series of negative experiences will make us paranoid if we continue to dwell on these negatives and if we do not redirect our concentration to positive things. A gentleman once told me that he was ripped off by almost every "friend" he had. Since his teenage years his "friends" and various other people took advantage of him. Year after year he was ripped off and betrayed by his "friends," usually regarding money he loaned to them and in small business deals, etc. As time went on and these negative experiences accumulated, he began to distrust everybody. But whenever he became better acquainted with a new-found "friend" and some mutual trust was established, it happened again—they just ripped him off again. It's like being beat with a baseball bat over and over again and again.

Without proper self-esteem this gentleman would've been the perfect candidate for severe depressions and possible suicide. Or imagine for him to go on a retaliation spree. He told me that he had to learn self-respect and he also had to learn forgiveness. While occasionally in situations he may be reminded on distinctive negative experiences, he has learned not to associate specific people with a specific negative experience. Therefore these negative experiences are only a mental point of reference for protection to possibly avoid potentially painful mistakes in the future. He told me that he has learned not to have a grudge against the people that have ripped him off. Before he learned the principle of forgiveness, he said, that more than once a thought crossed his mind about taking a shotgun and killing the individuals that had ripped him off in the past. Learning forgiveness is a process. This gentleman went through all the facts based in objective truth and he realized that money didn't really mean that much in terms of eternity. The lives of the people he once hated, because of what they've done to him, are much more valuable in the present than the money he lost doing business with them in the past. Yes, his experiences were sad experiences and were certainly painful— betrayal always hurts. Just being reminded of specific instances of betrayal can be devastating. But let's be realistic, we aren't so perfect either and during our lives we have betrayed people too, somehow, in one way or the other. Maybe our betrayal didn't center around finances and maybe we didn't even do it willfully, but nevertheless we've done it somehow. Maybe we forgot to meet a friend, or left a friend in the lurch, or in our selfishness we just said something that really hurt people involved in the conversation or innocent by-standers overhearing accidently the conversation.

I think betrayal in whatever form often happens not intentionally, but rather through carelessness and the lack of communication and definition regarding certain issues involved. Gossip is betrayal, too.

For one spouse to betray the other is certainly devastating and infidelity is a very difficult betrayal to deal with. As human beings we have the need to trust someone. Usually this someone for ultimate trust is the marriage partner. We'll discuss this subject later under the chapter "Love, Sex and Marriage."

WHAT DO YOU LIKE ABOUT YOURSELF?

Step in front of a mirror and look at yourself. First of all relax and don't think about anything else. Look at your face. Look into your eyes. Say "I love me" first whispering, then again say it out loud, really meaning it, but don't scream. Are your eyes getting watery? Do you feel the need to cry? If you do want to cry go ahead and cry a little bit. Crying can't hurt and it cleanses your tear canals. Crying is an emotional expression and even when it's undefined in an occasional instance it can be very helpful.

Go back to the mirror and once again look into your eyes and say "I love me." Look at yourself and see if you like anything physically on your body. Maybe it's your eyes which have seen a lot. Or maybe it's your skin, your hair, your lips, your nose, your ears, your profile, your fingers, or something else. Find something on or about you that you like. Usually the eyes will be good to look at and to look into.

Now think about it that you're a human being, wonderfully made. You were created. You are an absolute miracle. Physically it's unexplainable why your heart has been pumping for so many years and continues to do so every second. Take a deep breath slowly and enjoy breathing. Continue to look at yourself in the mirror. Blood is circulating throughout your body. If you know the God of the Bible thank Jesus Christ for what he has done in your life. If you don't know the God of the Bible, thank the God, Higher Power, Creator whatever you may currently call him, for making you the way you are and for giving you life day after day and breath by breath. By the way, I'm not ashamed to talk about God, because every person has something or someone that is their god in their life. In order to avoid and overcome depression, we must also discuss this subject later in detail. Not that I'm necessarily in favor of Marianne Williamson's bestselling 1992 book "A Return To Love," but for illustration purposes only, she began her book with a chapter on "Hell" followed by the second chapter entitled "God." These are vital subjects that not only cross our mind occasionally, but we must deal with them sooner or later.

Every building has an architect, a creator. For everything in life there is someone behind it who had the idea and created it. Of course, the human body is a very sophisticated "machine" and it's a miracle that each body continues to live for so many decades. With all the junk food that we eat and all the abuse our body has to endure, every single day of our life is truly an amazing miracle. Look into the mirror and check out how you function. Your fingers move, your mouth opens, your eyes can be closed, you can think thoughts, you can speak words. There is so much to discover about your miraculous body and none of the bodily functions are short of a miracle.

Love yourself just the way you are. Many people never do this exercise and never go in front of a mirror to say to themselves "I love me." They are ashamed, or are just preoccupied with something else and do not find a minute to practice the "I love me" exercise a couple of times a week or if possible once every day. You won't believe how your life and outlook for life is going to change—just by this little exercise. When you wake up in the morning go to the mirror and look into it saying out loud "I love me." Try it, it really works. Within a few days of practice you'll enjoy doing it and your self-esteem will grow. Find ways of being funny in front of the mirror and you'll fall in love with yourself. See, this is not the selfish love which is so often seen and talked about, but it's an objective love for oneself thanking our Creator for the miracle that we are. This is just the basic exercise and there is much more substance and depth to it which we'll also discuss in greater detail in just a little bit.

Usually in the morning you go to the mirror anyway. Take just a minute and practice the "I love me" exercise. It's really funny when you're brushing your teeth and you try to say "I love me." Say it a few times. Everybody can do it, it's free and only takes a minute. If you're single then after the "I love me" exercise give your teddy bear a big hug and ask him what he thinks, just for the fun of it. If you're married encourage your spouse to also practice the "I love me" exercise and soon you'll be able to say "I love you" to your mate from the bottom of your heart and really, really mean it. A bond of unconditional love will develop that will be very strong and boost each others' self-esteem, and your spouse will be protected from getting ideas about seeing someone else.

ACCEPTING YOUR IMPERFECTIONS

It's a fact that we are not perfect. Actually, we don't need to be perfect. We are not required to be perfect human beings. Yes, in business presentations and on the job we try to do everything just right, but it's not perfect. Perfection is not attainable. There is nothing wrong with the pursuit of excellence, but it's never going to be a hundred percent perfect.

Television and the media are always trying to impress us with perfectionism, but the mistakes still happen. The top fashion models and so called beauties are not perfect. Outward beauty is short lived, but inward beauty is long lasting. Don't be hyperspiritual either and just get married to inward beauty, instead it can be very helpful to see at least some outward beauty in your spouse. It's not that difficult to find some outward beauty in someone you love.

People are human beings and even the most "perfect" people have faults and make mistakes. We should eat right and keep our body somewhat in shape, but overweight people often go through severe depressive moods. They love eating. In the case of excessive eating habits there could be a problem somewhere inside the soul. Maybe it's the need to be loved, or just being unable to lose some weight. Not everybody is destined to have a slender body—our genetical format may very well allow us to be a little chubby. Only the odd television commercials and some infomercials consistently tell us that we need to lose weight, because only a so-called slim and healthy-looking body is accepted by society. Tests have shown that chubby people are often treated differently than perceived handsome looking individuals, who are seemingly treated better. Nowadays a healthy nutritional diet is important. But there is certainly nothing wrong with an occasional steak (Filet Mignon very well done only—just kidding) and a donut. Today, clothing stores have good selections in big and tall sizes. Sure, designer clothes remain to be made only for Barbie®-like bodies. You don't have to be concerned with your weight. For years I was able to wear one of the smallest men's sizes available. Shortly after I married Patricia, however, I gained a total of nearly eighty pounds over several years. I haven't really changed my eating habits. In fact, I eat healthier today than before I gained weight—it must be genetics. People waste a lot of money and many hours daily in an effort to lose weight and to go through this program and engage in that exercise. Exercise programs for up to an hour a day can't hurt, but so many people are left depressed when after they have tried everything under the sun, they just can't lose as much weight as they would like to. Accept your physical frame and if without excessive effort it works to lose a few pounds it's great, but don't strive doing it.

Only a few ladies are fashion models, which isn't a very desirable career anyway and therefore not every young lady has to be like them. Magazines always show off seemingly perfect bodies, but these bodies are not the standard. Love yourself just the way you are. Don't be a slob either, take care of yourself and make the best efforts to look nice. Nice and clean looking people are always received well no matter how much overweight they might be.

Choose the proper colors for your clothes. Most importantly, obtain some style whatever this may mean. Black almost always looks great. A white shirt or blouse under a black coat often enhances class. When I wear a black suit with a white shirt people frequently estimate my weight to be forty pounds less than what I actually weigh. In my personal case, an emphasis on light or bright colors will most likely make me appear chubbier than darker colors. You can always use lighter colors for smaller parts in your outfit, e.g. as mentioned before for shirts underneath the coat, or a scarf, etc. While it's not an issue and it depends solely on personal style, sometimes dark brown and most solid darker brown color shades are not amongst the most favored apparel colors for a business outfit. Next to black a solid dark blue will make a great choice. With dark blue as a dominant color in your outfit you'll be able to accentuate with white and blue striped shirts or blouses, and even a little yellow in a neck tie or a polo shirt could do wonders.

Shoes, if chosen carefully to match the outfit, can enhance the appearance additionally quite a bit. With just a little creativity you can look like a million dollars in a hurry and people won't notice that you're a little chubby, or at least it won't matter to them and you'll feel good, too.

Besides deodorant a little bit of quality perfume—

not too much though—can aid also to your appearance. Men could also use a little bit of cologne for a refreshing breeze, so to speak. Smell is truly a very important sense amongst our senses. Do you know that the smell of various things can literally initiate depressive moods, but also very encouraging positive motivation, at least in our thought process? Our memory system has various smells recorded and associates distinct odors with different positive or negative experiences. Think of fresh-baked bread, or fresh-cut flowers, etc. The choice of which perfume or cologne is best for you, of course, is a very personal decision. You may have to experiment a little bit to find the right scent for your type of desired personality. Only use a scent that you feel comfortable with and that stimulates positive thoughts to yourself. Try it and you'll see that it sure makes a difference on how you're treated in everyday life and how you personally will feel. As just mentioned before, a quality cologne can make people that come in contact with you feel comfortable and therefore relax the atmosphere within seconds.

The commercials tell us that men need to have hair on their heads, and being bald seemingly is a shame for whatever reason. This is definitely not true and I know several bald guys that look very cool. I know for sure that they would have good chances with the ladies, just by their appearance, if they'd give it a try.

Women are often reminded that they should have a certain size bosom. Many ladies have gone so far as to have surgery done for breast implants. While it is certainly understandable that for many breast-cancer patients it might be necessary to undergo this procedure for various reasons, it's very difficult to figure out why any healthy woman would have unnatural silicon implanted into her body just to enhance the appearance of her bosom. No husband should pressure his healthy wife to undergo such a procedure just for plain appearance sake. Once again, the magazines and television shows project to us what a perfect body supposedly looks like. But we're not obligated to look like these so-called perfect bodies. In fact, most human beings don't even come close to this perfect image.

Images of so called perfection are consistently floating over our television screen and are everywhere in the print media. Maybe it's time to turn off the television and to put aside the magazines. Once again, when we appear in public we should have a nice and clean appearance if we desire to come across as likeable nice people in order to leave a good first impression. Recently I had a really long workday from early in the morning until late at night. While taking a short break in the evening I drove quickly to the grocery store around the corner. Because of time I wasn't able to shave on that certain day. It was a little embarrassing to say the least when a nicely groomed and well dressed reporter from a major local newspaper recognized me in the grocery store and came towards me to shake my hand and to chat a little bit. Of course, there is no self-condemnation, but I'm now more careful to appear at least clean and neat when leaving my house.

We also need to be sensitive towards our spouses. A little makeup and lipstick to welcome your husband home after a day of hard work may do wonders—try it. A man shouldn't wear the same pair of jeans and the same old T-shirt every day. A selection of a few nice shirts will enhance the quality of life around the home, too. We just like to look at nice things and whatever we see is the first impression of anything we encounter. First impressions are important. To dress nicely feels good, too. It's called personal style. Of course, it's not something that we want to waste a lot of time and money on, but it's just a little practical thing on the side to make the mundane day a little more exciting, especially for the people around us.

Some people are crazy for clothes and more and more stuff gets loaded into their closet—that's definitely not what we're talking about. We don't derive our identity from what we wear, but nice things simply produce a friendlier atmosphere and environment for our eyes.

Besides physical imperfections there are all kinds of other imperfections. Maybe it's a problem with forgetting things or with being just a little careless regarding some details. For instance, maybe the cabinet doors in the kitchen aren't closed completely, or the clothes from the previous day aren't in the laundry room yet, but instead are spread across the bedroom floor for days to come. Or maybe the coffee mug has been left in the car overnight and now the car smells really bad. Or maybe the gum was placed temporarily on the tablecloth a few days ago, and now the gum can no longer be removed easily and in fact has become part of the tablecloth. I know people that continuously let their supply of soap, toilet paper, milk, bread, etc. run out. It's not limitations on their budget which is the problem, but just their inability of keeping track of their stock of a few important basic items. Some people I know will always wait until the last minute to take care of things. Of course, it's not rare that the certain thing which they were supposed to take care of already days ago, finally just won't get done, or only to some extent. A husband once told me that he had to wait four years for his wife to finish the length of a pair of pants he bought. By the time he got his pants they didn't fit in the waist anymore. When he emphasized his wish to finally receive his pants it only took the wife ten minutes to do this simple job.

Each one of us has imperfections. Some things we might be able to improve without striving, but regarding many things we may just be unable to improve or change anything. For whatever reason certain imperfections are stuck with us. We not only need to accept the unchangeable imperfections on and in us, but we must also learn to accept other people with their multitude of imperfections. Life will be much easier and friendlier for us and the world around us if we do not impose our relative standard of perfection upon others or ourselves.

It is understood that at work the boss may demand a great job performance from an employee and often there is little room for mistakes. Rarely, however, does a boss require absolute perfection. While we should do the very best job possible, we cannot let ourselves become slaves to this relative standard of perfection. In some jobs certain things have to be accurate and complete, otherwise e.g. the construction of a building may have problems sooner or later. But if you're trained in a certain professional area, because you like this type or that kind of work, then you'll be able to do an excellent job without any doubt, which will satisfy all expectations of your boss. There's a proper balance to these things. Don't be afraid to make mistakes, because this very fear will cause you to make even more mistakes. You have certain qualifications and that's why you've been put on a certain job and that's why you're able to do it just "perfectly."

MAKING TIME FOR YOURSELF

In all that's going on day after day, it's crucial to take some time off for yourself. At least an hour a day should be scheduled just for yourself. Also purpose to have one day or at least an afternoon and evening off once a week. It can be difficult to find time for yourself when you have a professional career. Time is also scarce for a homemaker with three or four small children who consistently need attention.

If you don't take time off for yourself, you're a

candidate for depression, anxiety, stress, heart attack and the burnout syndrome. Once in my life I worked virtually day and night for ten months consistently—really eighteen-hour workdays, seven days a week. I didn't make time for myself to relax nor did I make a provision to spend any quality time with my family. It was ludicrous, and while making a lot of money during this ten-months period it nearly cost me my marriage and almost my life. I continue to like my work a lot and there will always be certain deadlines, but things need to be balanced and a proper time management can be very helpful. It's never worth it to become a true workaholic to jeopardize your health and inner peace, or to destroy your marriage, family life or other meaningful relationships.

A time for yourself usually doesn't make itself available automatically. You must schedule it. There are a lot of distractions that may rob us of quality time for ourselves. In the evening instead of watching television or reading the paper or a magazine, or playing a video game, etc., simply sit down in your favorite chair and think and do absolutely nothing. It's not wasted time, in fact, it's a powerful time of regeneration. An appreciative attitude for life with thankfulness for every breath we take, can be tremendously helpful. Some details of life can become major distractions and produce undefined discontentment, and that's also why a continuous positive attitude is so very important.

If we make quality time for ourselves, many things that happened during the day won't be that serious anymore and won't be a problem like before. Stress is a killer, and while nowadays most of us may have a very busy schedule, never let yourself be put under stress. Proper time management can help a lot. Whenever we eat breakfast, lunch or dinner, we must relax—and shouldn't be in a rush to finish our plate. For many reasons it's much better to eat less and throw away leftovers than to eat everything in a hurry causing your stomach to work twice as hard.

In our hectic world, relaxation is truly a lost art. Whenever we're in a hurry we must concentrate much more and the continuous tension will drive us to the edge. It's not healthy to live that way, because of an anxious and stressful lifestyle our life can and probably will be shortened by several years. I know life is short and things need to get done, but we shouldn't rush things beyond a relatively normal and acceptable pace— whatever this may mean in each individual case and situation. If you sit down and mentally schedule your day in fifteen to thirty-minute increments you're able to accomplish much more than when you're trying to do everything at once, right now.

We once conducted an interesting efficiency experiment. One of our small companies had six employees and I decided to lay off all of them. Instead, I was trying to do the job of half a dozen full-time employees alone. The result was phenomenal. I personally had to work really hard and long hours. By applying distinctive principles of time and efficiency management, I by myself, doing all of the work alone, was able to achieve even more than what the whole crew together was able to accomplish. Not only did I save myself the energy to explain everything over and over again, it also was healthy to my nervous system, because all mistakes that were made were mine and we didn't have to figure out who is responsible for this or that mistake. By the way, all the good people I had working for me back then, were very good to excellent employees and they were loyal to the company. I don't think anybody could have done a much better job than they did. But still, our experiment proved to be very successful also regarding the bottom line of the financial performance.

Driving anywhere exactly by the legal speed limit posted we'll always encounter this one car in the rear-view mirror that is all of a sudden seemingly glued to the rear end of our car. Being intimidated by this behavior could produce speeding tickets and definitely unnecessary stress for yourself. If this happens I make it a habit not to look into my rearview mirror. That certain individual behind me will start calling me names and whatever, but it's not my problem. It's that certain individual's problem and this is a burden I'm not willing to carry. Therefore I don't look into the rearview mirror and I ignore this type of foolish and childish behavior. People like that have to learn to relax. I'm not going to jeopardize my own safety or the safety of anyone else, and I don't share in the unnecessary stress of others, just because someone has an unresolved achievement problem for whatever reason. Unless it's a genuine life-or-death emergency there is nothing in the world that should lead us into a stressful behavior—and definitely not on the road. Let him honk his horn—he better get hold of this book.

In traffic you can really do a lot of exercise regarding patience and giving grace to others. Right there it is revealed how selfish and self-centered people really are and how much they respect the life of others. It's also easy to tell the quality and level of their self-esteem.

Many chief executives work really a lot. They find it difficult to take some time off for themselves, but they've got to do it. Otherwise they won't live fulfilled lives; a mid-life crisis may occur, the marriage will suffer and the relationship to their kids will be damaged. All of this is in the pursuit of getting more and more money to, in effect, purchase and afford some sort of happiness and convenience in the end. By buying more and more and better and better things, genuine happiness can't be obtained. There is, of course, nothing against making millions and millions of dollars as long as we can, but there needs to be a certain balance to all of this, otherwise we won't have the opportunities to enjoy any of the financial blessings, or any other blessings.

A homemaker, too, has a lot of work to do and most of the time her work isn't rewarded directly financially by a weekly or monthly paycheck. Still, the family cannot become an idol or excuse for not taking care of yourself. This could cause a burnout resulting in devastating consequences that may never be healed, or may take years to cure. Even a housewife can make time for herself to relax and to be regenerated.

Read a book, take a walk, sit around and just look into the sky or over the fields. Enjoy every breath that you take—don't be familiar with life. Life is so fragile and we must thank our Creator for what He has given us. Not the rat race nor any money in the world can come close to the enjoyment of a beautiful blue sky, a sunset, or the stars and the moon on a clear summer night. Think of the fragrance after the rain, or of the beauty of fresh snow, the vista of a mountain range, or the sound of the ocean as waves are rolling onto the beach, the smile of a baby, the laughter and inner joy of young children, or the utmost culinary experience of a superb steak or blackened salmon. The freedom and inner healing these things produce and provide to the careful observer are indescribable, because these things are truly blessings.

On the other hand I do not disagree that it is a tremendous experience and even a rush at making a whole bunch of money in a very short period of time. Therefore enabling you to buy whatever your heart desires. With it, however, comes some type of bondage and often a lot of worries.

I think you understand that we're not suggesting a selfish behavior in just living for ourselves egotistically. In order to function properly as human beings we must make time in our very busy schedules to regenerate ourselves and to enter into at least short periods of appreciation for our lives and the lives of others on a daily basis. Applying this principle will also make us more sensitive to the needs of others and more under-standing, living life more extensively and intensely than before. During this time for ourselves we should never entertain subjective or negative thoughts. Self-pity is a killer, too. Introspection and trying to figure out why we've reacted this way or that way, and why we've done things in this manner and not otherwise, etc. will always lead to stress, anxiety and finally right into depression. As mentioned previously, the past has already gone and is history, and therefore it cannot be changed anymore. We don't need to figure out what we could have done differently to produce other effects or results—it's no longer an issue.

This distinctive time for yourself needs to be a valuable quality time to ponder positive thoughts in appreciation of many various things. That's why it's so helpful to take a look at nature. Nature is overwhelming and if we're willing to be relaxed we can really be energized just by appreciating nature and therefore thanking the Creator for what He has created and given us. He has made it available to us free of charge for our sole enjoyment. Don't take anything for granted.

In this process of taking time for ourselves we will also learn to make time for our loved ones. Yes, we must spend time alone with our spouses, and we must also spend time together as a family. Every child needs our specific care and attention. Hugging, too, is a very important practice and we must say to our mate and children that we love them on a daily basis. Taking and making time for ourselves and for our relationships in the family will produce a harmonious flow of love while strengthening relationships. Practiced properly it will bring utmost fulfillment to our lives and impart something very special into the lives of our loved ones. When we were small children our parents took care of us and when they get older they may need our help. Do we really appreciate life so that we truly care for each other?

It's only in the present that we can experience time and time is very valuable—we must treasure it and invest it properly. Every minute is only available once. We can use time to make an eternal investment in the lives of others resulting in eternal benefits for them and ourselves. Or instead we can choose to waste our precious time in the pursuit of hunting after the temporal things that only give us limited satisfaction for the moment.

Whatever our choice may be, time is a valuable treasure entrusted to each one of us and some day we'll be held accountable for our stewardship regarding this treasure.

3

LOVE, SEX AND MARRIAGE

This theme is certainly a very hot and important subject. What is love? How much sex is enough? And is marriage forever?

DEFINITION OF LOVE

In the English language we have basically only one word for love. More precise languages such as the Koine Greek have various words ascribed to the different types of love. The Koine Greek has basically four words for love each with a specific meaning. Therefore love is specifically defined and this provides a more precise understanding of love than our general English word for love. These four basic meanings in the Koine Greek are:

(a) A passionate erotic love originally derived from the Greek god of love who was called "Eros;"

(b) A type of family love or affection amongst family members;

(c) A friendship love or special affection amongst friends;

(d) Agape love which is God's unconditional love and the highest form of love in which the object of this love is loved unconditionally, disregarding the response or rejection of this love by the object.

To discuss this theme effectively these basic definitions on love are very helpful so that we can define and understand what we're talking about. Nowadays we can find plenty of references to erotic love almost everywhere. Sensuality has penetrated our society from A to Z. Sadly enough sensuality improperly applied destroys the soul. Erotic love has it's place and is very important in the marital union. Many people, however, have a distorted and degenerate sex life. While there is still a subconscious moral sense of what's right and wrong, there is hardly any definition, or should we say standard, that's communicated in our western world today.

To discuss this subject properly and to get the right picture of what love really is and to see its characteristics and nature we must also consult objective truth which says the following about love:

> "Love endures long and is patient and kind; love never is envious nor boils over with jealousy, is not boastful or vainglorious, does not display itself haughtily. It is not conceited (arrogant and inflated with pride); it is not rude (unmannerly) and does not act unbecomingly. Love (God's love in us) does not insist on its own rights or its own way, for it is not self-seeking; it is not touchy or fretful or resentful; it takes no account of the evil done to it [it pays no attention to a suffered wrong]. It does not rejoice at injustice and unrighteousness, but rejoices when right and truth prevail. Love bears up under anything and everything that comes, is ever ready to believe the best of every person, its hopes are fadeless under all circumstances, and it endures everything [without weakening]. Love never fails [never fades out or becomes obsolete or comes to an end]."[1]

Considering this definition of perfect love, it's very

obvious that we ourselves in our own efforts and characteristics as human beings are absolutely incapable of
producing this type of love. Pure love is of supernatural
origin and this type of love has energy and the power to
produce tremendous responses. This true love has an
impact upon society, but we're unable to produce this
type of love within our own efforts. This beautiful and
effective love must be received from Someone who has
Himself intrinsically the characteristics of this love and
who is actually Love Himself. It's normal to ascribe this
attribute and the characteristics of this type of love to
God, no matter what your religious affiliation, beliefs,
or definition of God might be, and even if your God is
abstract and only a so called Higher Power. But if your
God has the characteristics of pure love just described,
then your God is not really abstract anymore, but step
by step becomes a very personal God to you.

We can freely receive this love from God, if we would
like to have it, as objective truth reveals, "Because the
love of God has been poured out within our hearts
through the Holy Spirit who was given to us."[2]

1   1 Corinthians 13:4-8, The Amplified Bible

2   Romans 5:5, NASB

MARRIAGE AND INFIDELITY

Back in the early sixties in Austria and other parts of Central Europe, divorces were almost unheard of and it was something very rare. Today, the moral standards regarding sexuality and marriage, e.g. in Austria and other European countries have been virtually erased and dropped significantly in comparison to even a type of a degenerate Sodom-and-Gomorrah level. In almost all of the western world there are often more divorces than marriages that stay together. This trend alone tells us that there is something essentially wrong with society. Is it a lack of commitment? Do we just go by what feels good for "Me" momentarily? Is it finally the penetration and saturation of a liberal philosophy which has no values, standards or rules and in which anything goes? Or is it a deep need inside the soul that is undefined and we're trying to fill this insatiable desire with anything we think could be the answer and seems best for us at the moment?

Infidelity is a very hurtful type of betrayal. Marriage is based on trust. While in the world out there it's very difficult to trust someone wholeheartedly, the marital union should remain a safe haven of unconditional mutual trust. When this trust has been violated, then insecurity, bitterness and depression may find an open door. Marriage is a commitment for a lifetime. Yes, there'll be disagreements and arguments and never ever is the verbal or even physical abuse of a spouse justified. Physical and verbal abuses are also not justified in society or everyday life. An abusive person testifies to their lack of self-esteem and lack of respect for human life.

Sadly enough, divorces happen and in some cases it's almost inevitable. In our lives we all make mistakes and when it comes to marriage we may have chosen the wrong partner or got married for the wrong reasons. But still, the marriage vows are for a lifetime and there are only a few cases in which a separation could be justified. In most cases a continuous physically abusive relationship must be separated until the physically abusive spouse is evidently healed from such practices. Even an isolated case of physical confrontation should never happen and especially men must learn to keep their cool. A physical confrontation is not an option, except, of course, in the case of necessary self-defense including when our children need immediate protection from such assaults. In the case of infidelity, especially when it's a habitual practice, it's understandable that the victimized mate may seek a divorce. As we've just discussed, infidelity is a very painful type of betrayal. A single isolated case of infidelity may have been a mistake and depending on the circumstances, etc. it certainly will also depend on the capacity of forgiveness of the victimized spouse, if this marriage has a chance for continuation.

While polygamy may not be a widespread practice in its "traditional" sense anymore, it still exists in many different forms in the Middle East and various parts of the world and even here in North America. Polygamy is never justified—no matter what type of religious beliefs people may have and use trying to justify this type of a degenerate lifestyle.

The most popular polygamous group in North America were the Mormons (Church of Jesus Christ of Latter-day Saints) who used to practice polygamy based on their religious beliefs. While the Mormons seemingly no longer have the practice of polygamy in the present time, they justified their former practice by special religious revelations. In such case polygamy was never admitted to having been a wrongful practice. Instead it is justified as an absolutely correct practice during a certain time period because of religious beliefs or "special" revelations. This continues to leave the door wide open to the possibility of reinstating the practice of polygamy and all kinds of other weird practices at some time in the future, if some of their high-ranking leaders would receive such strange revelations some day in the future.

Today, the Mormons portray themselves in promotions to be a family oriented group. And I'm sure that there are many sincere Mormons with very good intentions that probably really desire to follow God. But, pardon me for asking, how can anybody portray themselves to have a family emphasis with the history and background of polygamy like the Mormons do? This practice certainly did a lot of harm to the American family and has set a terrible example regarding what marriage should be. It's absolutely understood that if someone would come to their senses and would admit that such practices were wrong and sinful, and therefore is repentant and remorseful of such devastating practices, it would no longer be an issue and it's gone and it would be forgotten. But remember, while the Mormons may not practice polygamy today, they continue to justify polygamy in their history as a proper lifestyle for that certain time period, and they do not consider it to have been a wrongful practice.

Nobody can be safe in cults and sects that accept "new" revelations from people and even so-called angels if these revelations are not based on the Word of God, the Bible. The innocence and integrity of each individual in such cults is at risk and prone to be violated even in the most intimate private areas of their life. Just for the record, we must state that such groups and cults misinterpret certain passages from the Bible, in which a few cases of polygamy are mentioned, to justify their behavior and polygamous practices. When studying these passages and the whole context and nature of the Bible carefully, it's not that difficult to discover that God certainly never sanctioned polygamy as a desirous or correct practice or lifestyle. Instead we find in all such cases of polygamous instances in the Bible, that such behavior was associated with depression, betrayal, jealousy, hatred, devastation, family breakups and even murder. In the Bible, God clearly intended a monogamous marriage—one husband and one wife—there is no question about it, it's crystal clear.

Where does infidelity start? We have to realize that we're basically self-centered individuals and while being enabled through our soul power to do human good, we're just not the good human beings many want us to believe we are. In fact, objective truth explains the state of humanity saying that "The heart is deceitful above all things, and desperately wicked: who can know it?"₁ and "There is none righteous, no, not one: . . . there is none that doeth good, no, not one."₂ As we grew up in society we were influenced consistently since we were little kids. Adults provide examples of the so-called real world. Bad and wrong influences may energize our desperately wicked state in one area more than in another.

Frequently relationship psychologists will tell us that masturbation is just another tolerated form of sexuality. The thought of such activity is projected by various forms of communication from so-called "qualified" and also from unqualified sources. As we come into the teenage years premarital sex is explained by many as a gathering of sexual experiences and that it's normal to have such experiences. They say, "Considering everything, sex is natural and it's normal to have sexual desires." In fact, this is true. Nevertheless, we must not express our sexual desires in an uncontrolled manner. There is an appropriate application for sex. Today, condoms are being distributed in public schools to sanction premarital sexual activities as legitimate. Once we become adults and are entering the mid-twenties and sadly enough have had some or more sexual experiences, and by chance have not contracted AIDS just yet, then we tend to get married. What's the true reason or motive why we get married? Do we really get married because of all four basic aspects of love, or is it just an erotic desire and maybe because of some coincidental circumstances? Once married we're being indoctrinated by movies, television and magazines that extramarital sexual relations are okay and may even add some juice to our marriage. It's truly insane. Nowadays, Hollywood hardly ever produces a motion picture that depicts a traditional family in which the marriage is functioning properly. In the movies we almost always find divorces and extramarital affairs. It is sad to observe, that when a spouse has a problem with this philosophy and if sex may be seemingly better with someone else, a divorce is on the horizon—after all, we want to get the best out of our short life.

Infidelity, adultery and fornication start in the mind before any physical act is committed. The sad thing is that once these things take place in the mind the destruction of the soul is in progress. That's also why we desperately need objective truth which is the only remedy to heal our soul.

1   Jeremiah 17:9, KJV

2   Romans 3:10, 12, KJV

HOMOSEXUALITY

Along the way we're also confronted with perverted sex like homosexuality. Let us say this, that never ever should any reader feel condemned by anything we've written in this book. While we may not agree with certain actions, practices and lifestyles, because of the tremendous harm these things cause, we certainly never ever condemn the individual who does these things or is actually living in such a lifestyle. You are very special and you're accepted just the way you are. You don't have to change, because you may not want to change or you may not be able to change by your own strength. So, please, relax and just read on, because we're here to help you and certainly don't want to beat up on you. We don't judge you and we don't accuse you, so don't take certain things personal when we discuss these activities, practices and lifestyles, even though these things may affect you currently and immediately.

Certain experts often want to make us believe that people are born to be homosexuals. That's a lie. Nobody has ever been born a homosexual. Homosexuality is a choice. At first the homosexual act seems strange and odd and guilt comes in, but the more often the homosexual act is repeated, which each time is a choice, the easier it gets to do this act and to make this perverted choice.

It's like with everything else. There is the first cigarette and there is the first drink—and it's a choice which we individually make. First we smoke one cigarette and we almost cough ourselves to death, but the more often we practice smoking the easier it will become. Every single time we inhale the smoke, we will effectively take away at least five breaths of our life. Alcohol and drugs are the same. First we have a drink and it tastes ugly, but the more often we do it the more we seemingly like it. After all it's a cool thing to do the commercials tell us, not letting us know that we become chemically dependent on this stuff. Nevertheless, the end of various habits and unnatural practices as just described is self-destruction. Depression won't go away and will be escorting these individuals to the bitter end. It will also harm the loved ones around them. We've seen it happen over and over again.

While I've always been straight throughout my life, I've had many homosexual and lesbian friends. Some of them were very good friends of mine and I watched their lives for years and they shared their thoughts with me. I dare to say that I understand what they were going through. I've also seen what happens when they're alone at home and when they do some soul searching—it's sad. Suicidal tendencies and depression are consistently present, only to hide it for another day when tomorrow they're back again with their own crowd.

Do we condemn the individual that has made terrible choices and is seemingly hooked on these unnatural things? No, never, because we want to help them and we wouldn't make it an issue if we met with someone living in such a lifestyle—it really wouldn't matter and it's not an issue, because we all have one thing or the other that we do and practice, and that we may even enjoy, but is just not good for us. We must mention these things for the general reader to illustrate that certain things are destructive and are definitely not a solution to heal depression, etc. We certainly care about every person that fell victim to a degenerate lifestyle. Of course, there is hope for everybody and their miserable life can be changed in a moment. You may not see it yet or realize it that this is what's really going on in your life. A great life is just a choice away, and it's not a very difficult choice to make. Objective truth will tenderly motivate us to make positive choices and the rest will fall into place automatically.

SEXUAL ENCOUNTERS

But let's go back to discuss the sex problem in the marriage. All the misguided and perverted sex practices and images destroy the soul gradually. We're often incapacitated to have good functioning relationships and individuals are left empty inside, prone to be depressed.

Let's leave the fact aside that most people get married for the wrong reasons. What happens once two people get married? If they had premarital sex, wounds have been carved into their soul. Eventual sexual incompatibility is almost inevitable. All of a sudden, the pressures of life are very real. No longer does the wife dream of her husband being the white knight or the saving prince, even though she wishes that he would be. And the wife no longer is the unreachable and untouchable beauty queen, but now there is no makeup on her face in the morning. Babies may be crying in the background and a mountain of bills must be paid month after month. There is pressure at the workplace to perform successfully day in and day out. Looking at the whole picture, it's not that easy to advance in this world system with the accumulation of common status symbols that seemingly promise us the continuation of a pseudo-happiness for a little longer.

The frequency of sex is reduced dramatically and it isn't as exciting as it used to be. Some married women consider sex to be a marital duty now and obviously the overwhelming joy and expectations are gone. Sex should actually produce tremendous bonding between the married couple. If this doesn't happen both become sexually dissatisfied on the lookout for greener pastures to rekindle their desires they once experienced before marriage. Frequently it's dragging on for years and years, most likely resulting in divorce. Besides destroying themselves the children are innocent victims, only left with terrible examples of how a marriage and relationship shouldn't be. But who cares, "they'll manage," we think, as long as we live in the illusion of being seemingly happy, which we aren't, of course.

Men are often insensitive to their wives when they come home after a day of hard work. They may want dinner to be ready the moment they enter the home. But also they may want sex on a quicky instead of going through romantic foreplay. This often turns women off, because they want the whole package with romance, etc. and they may feel used if they don't get it. If the husband works hard and loves you, even though he may not show it very often with gestures such as bringing you flowers, etc., but nevertheless he loves you from the bottom of his heart, please, never feel used, because that will eat you up and ultimately ruin your marriage. He is your husband and you should be happy that he is faithful, that he doesn't abuse you and that he works very hard to provide for you and the family. From the bottom of his heart he loves you, even though he might be insensitive at times.

Tell him occasionally that you remember how wonderful it was when he brought flowers to your doorstep before you both were married and he may begin to bring you flowers more often now and then. Tell him about the times you both were sitting on the front porch looking at the moon and counting the stars and you'll be doing this again occasionally. A man needs the security of knowing that his wife loves him and that she knows that he really loves her, otherwise he'll be very insecure and this may cause even more problems.

A nagging wife is a pain in the neck. A nagging husband, too. Playing the blame game and trying to find fault with each other is a frustrating and destructive experience. Of course, sex won't be any fun if the screaming and hollering goes on for hours day after day. We must learn to accept the imperfections of others, especially the imperfections of our spouse—nobody is perfect. As explained in a previous chapter as we learn to love ourselves, including accepting our imperfections, we will also learn in this process to love others just the way they are, including accepting their imperfections. Sure, certain things will be annoying, but let's look at these things as part of life and as an exciting experience. Forgiving one another will do wonders and relax the atmosphere bringing kindness and love to a room, house and family, and even to the workplace. To go on a feeding frenzy about little details will only charge the atmosphere with hate, hurt and destruction. Imagine the impact such shouting wars have on our children. They'll be left insecure, confused and without the experience of love, and they'll feel unloved and unwanted. We too, as adults, will suffer the same consequences of such unnecessary confrontations and will become even more depressed. As just mentioned, nobody is perfect, and certain situations may arise where there is a disagreement, but it can be discussed quietly, or in some cases it simply must be left alone as we let go of it.

In today's society it is not uncommon that the wife takes on a job, too. While financially it may be helpful, it could put a lot of strain on a relationship, especially within a young marriage when small children come along. It's important not to become burnouts and to simply live a realistic affordable lifestyle. To keep up with the projected images what you should be and what you should have is ludicrous as mentioned before and produces a lot of unnecessary stress.

Stay simple, let the man be the head of the household. The woman is a helpmate, but both are equal in every sense of the word and count just the same. But like in everything else there is a certain order to avoid chaos. Every corporation and organization has a table of organization. In a company there is a president, executive manager, supervisor, secretaries and all kinds of employees each assigned to a different task. The boss will make the decisions, but left to himself alone would be unable to accomplish the corporate task of reaching the business goals and the desired achievements. Every employee is needed in his or her function to make a company work and to acquire corporate success.

When it comes to sports the team concept is even more evident. There is only one coach and not every player can be in a quarterback position. Every player though has a function and only together as a team will they be able to win. Only one can be the driver of a race car, but it sure takes the effort of a whole group of mechanics and technicians to finish a race. In music the same structure is prevalent. Somebody must be the lead singer while the band takes care of the musical instruments and may only get involved in the singing occasionally, e.g. in choruses for backup, etc.

In the home when the husband-and-wife team is functioning properly, even though they may disagree in some areas or regarding some opinions, etc. things will work out fine and together as a team they'll succeed.

To understand this subject better we must know

that women have the beautiful gift of responding, while men are initiators. That's why the husband is normally the leader of the home, not to lord over his wife or to enslave her and the children, but to be a servant. A leader has to be a servant first in order to be a good leader. This means that the leader is willing to literally lay down his life for the family. It's easy to follow a leader when he's your servant, ready to encourage you and to build you up and to serve you. Throughout life we have the authority principle. This means that someone or something must be in charge and for our own benefit we must respect that authority. Laws, rules and certain standards are given and established to protect life and to provide freedom for everybody to have a chance to potentially live a fulfilled life in a safe environment. No wife should become a robot, but instead is a coequal individual. Both, husband and wife, should learn to live in harmony with each other, which may reach into every area of life.

Sex in the marital union is truly a phenomenal experience. It is regenerating and this intimacy will build a very strong bond between husband and wife. It's the highest form of physical unity that can be experienced by human beings on earth. When, for no physical or health reasons, sexual activity in the marriage ceases, pressure and frustration will be build up. That's when tension will accumulate and certain things will become out of sync, so to speak. Sex is only a part of marriage, but it surely is a vital part because of the regenerating effect sex has and the intensified experience of love and unity. If women would look at sex with their marriage partner as a regenerating experience, they would never feel used.

The frequency of sex depends solely on the married couple. We would say that whenever one spouse would like to have sex it's time for it. There should be reason for concern when the sexual activity ceases steadily with a tendency to weaken the frequency even further. This, of course, supposing that both parties are physically in a healthy condition. Women should not use sex as a weapon to blackmail their husband, because that is a sure bet to end your marriage in a hurry. The attitude about the whole subject of sex in marriage needs to be examined. Yes, at times men may come across as being lustful and it may seem that they must have sex right away. Usually women aren't having sex just because of duty, but are certainly enjoying sex, too. Regarding sex, women should obtain an attitude that sex is an exciting experience and pleasure, and that they, too, really want sex.

Forget about listening to these feminists which more often than not have a weird concept about sex and marriage, and occasionally have lesbian tendencies. Often their lives are ruined and they have no family, and they are just in need of a support group to confirm their wrong choices. These feminists could have a great husband and a well functioning family, too, if they would just humble themselves and become available to listen to objective truth. Often, they hide behind their wall of men-hating agenda, which testifies to their lack of self-esteem. They're hurtful and buried in their self-pity which traumatizes females even to a much greater extent while entering into a severe personal identity crisis. To be part of such a group or movement could potentially destroy your marriage and doesn't help you. We clearly understand that rape is a terrible crime and should be punished severely. If a woman has become the victim of rape, she is not the guilty party, but she has been severely violated. When a woman is assaulted she should not be afraid to hit the guy frequently between the legs into his private parts as violently as possible. This will disable him potentially for several minutes and possibly discourage him to proceed with the crime, and could provide the victim with enough time to escape the situation.

At the workplace women sometimes encounter sexual harassment. A boss may try to intimidate women to have sex with him—we've all heard of it, seen reports about it, and probably have experienced it. Women should never give in to any kind of such pressure—there'll always be another job. Here are a few hints to women that may reduce the potential risk of rape and sexual harassment. If in any way possible dress modestly. While women are more likely to be stimulated by touch, men are stimulated by sight. Therefore avoid wearing tight and very short skirts. A blouse or shirt shouldn't be too tight either nor should the cut be low in the front, so that incidents of baring too much of your bosom are avoided. While we like to create a friendly environment, especially at the workplace, women should be careful not to be too overly friendly. A woman can very easily send false signals and therefore stimulate a man. Flirting is certainly not appropriate for married people, unless it's between husband and wife, because flirting works as a stimulant. Obviously, it's up to each person what to do and how to conduct themselves, but certain negative consequences and various problems can be avoided by applying just a few practical and simple techniques.

While we won't discuss sexual practices in this book, the marriage bed allows husband and wife to experiment and enjoy their sexual desires on a broad scale. Pornography should never find the way into any house. While it may be stimulating momentarily, ultimately pornographic material endorses infidelity and always excludes the whole spectrum of love while concentrating just on the area of erotic love with it's self-centered attention of self-gratification.

Perverted sex, of course, is out of the question, which is also frequently endorsed by these pornographic materials. Regarding sexual practices both parties need to feel comfortable with what they're doing in the marriage bed. They shouldn't be afraid of experimenting with all kinds of general sexual practices, which they think may be sexually fulfilling for both of them. Even though there is a learning period, no spouse should ever be forced to do things that they feel uncomfortable with, because it could traumatize them to some extent, and it may inhibit the enjoyment of sexual activities in the future. That's also why husband and wife shouldn't be ashamed to talk about distinctive practices to each other. Communication is a vital part to make sex a truly memorable and exciting experience. Self-respect and respect for each other must remain intact at all times. Properly done each spouse will be occupied with the arousal and sexual fulfillment of the other as the woman will finally give in and enjoy her orgasm first.

Don't be occupied with the claim or rather theory of multiple orgasms in a row which some sex therapists and magazine articles falsely propagate to be a possible achievement. It's almost never possible to have multiple orgasms within a relatively short period of time. Enjoy the romantic and erotic foreplay, if any, and enjoy the one orgasm at this certain sexual encounter and you'll be fulfilled. Should another sexual encounter follow treat it as a new incident and a fresh experience. Neither husband nor wife should feel pressured to stage a performance. Sex is given primarily for enjoyment and has a regenerating effect. The sexual act should always be an exciting, fun, liberating, unifying and regenerating experience.

4

OBJECTIVE TRUTH

Having already mentioned the importance of objective truth in this book, it surely makes sense to discuss objective truth in detail.

OBJECTIVE TRUTH DEFINED

Objective truth is the complete guide and key to understanding and solving all problems that exist. But what is objective truth and where can we find it? According to dictionaries the words "objective" and "objectivity" mean actually existing, real, not subjective, dealing with the truth and facts without distortion by feelings, opinions, or prejudice. The word "truth" speaks of authenticity, genuineness, veracity, accuracy, actuality and reality. Objective truth does not leave room for private interpretations, but excludes error and therefore is absolutely perfect. No matter how we personally feel about it or what opinions others may bring against objective truth, the absolute reality and accuracy of objective truth will never change. Objective truth has been established and is anchored in eternity past and will remain the same unchanged in the present and throughout all eternity to come in the future indefinitely. God says about objective truth that "Heaven and earth shall pass away, but my words shall not pass away."[1] "Forever, O Lord, Thy word is settled in heaven."[2]

You may say, "Gee, that's a little over my head," but it doesn't have to be that way and you can simply lean back and relax and enjoy that there is such a thing as objective truth.

[1]   Matthew 24:35, KJV
[2]   Psalm 119:89, NASB

HOW DOES OBJECTIVE TRUTH WORK?

Objective truth provides not only a universal guideline about every subject and for everything in the universe, but also provides explanation and energy and power to live a fulfilled life on earth and throughout eternity. We may not grasp it entirely, but eternity never had a beginning and never has an ending—it will go on forever and ever, billions and billions of years from now eternity will still be as vibrant as it has always been.

Most things in life are finite. Meaning that all things have limitations and a certain time limit and therefore have an end. Virtually all things in the temporal value system including our own earthly life are just a vapor, here today and gone tomorrow. Currently, nearly six billion people live on our planet. The average human life span of seventy years is virtually nothing in comparison to eternity.

Objective truth has not been established to hurt anyone, but instead it should be viewed as the ultimate perfect counsel of wisdom. Objective truth is given to heal us and to deliver us from our destructions. When a person discovers objective truth, it's the best thing that could have happened to an individual. Objective truth will set a person free and even secure the eternal destiny of such an individual. "And you shall know the truth, and the truth shall make you free."[1]

Because each person has a free will, objective truth will never force itself upon an individual. Every person in the world is equipped with a free will. Objective truth will only present itself gently and suggest that it is a good thing for a human being to accept objective truth as a counselor, a wise friend and a companion. Objective truth will lead people and motivate them to accept objective truth for their own best, but eventually it is the free volition of each person that will have to make a decision to accept or reject objective truth.

1   John 8:32, NASB

THE AUTHORITY OF OBJECTIVE TRUTH

All human philosophies are limited to the imaginations and intellectual capacity of mankind. These philosophies provide ideas and theories that may be more or less beneficial to an individual. Objective truth, however, is not only limitless because of its supernatural origin, but will always in every aspect be beneficial to every person who is willing to accept it. First, it may only be in a certain area that we accept objective truth, but as we see objective truth actively perform and show us things we never thought existed and could be possible, step by step we will trust objective truth more and more, and make it our very personal treasure.

It is very difficult to explain objective truth in words to someone who has never consciously seen or experienced the miraculous power of objective truth in action. We're not talking about hocus-pocus or deceitful magical tricks nor are we talking about some undefined mysterious emotional experience which can only be obtained by a select group of people. As we've explained in the beginning of this chapter, objective truth does not necessarily have anything to do with personal feelings or opinions, even though objective truth will produce healthy emotions and therefore desirable and beneficial responses. Objective truth is available to all, no matter what color their skin, what language they speak, what size of intellectual capacity they might have, what social class they belong to, or what nationality they are.

Objective truth must be of supernatural origin,

because mankind in itself is unable to produce something so perfect for every area and aspect of life. We may say that objective truth must be of divine origin, because only a perfect being like God, the Creator, is able to produce and establish objective truth without failing and without error.

As we've been fed subjectivity throughout most of our life, objective truth may seem a little strange at first to our perception. Thoughts of objective truth are different and are usually contrary to a subjective system of thought. Subjectivity is incomplete and vague, but objective truth is absolute, complete and precise. It's like the light bulb just went on and everything regarding distinctive subjects are all of a sudden crystal clear. No more questions remain—objective truth is overwhelming. As we understand one area we're interested to know more about another area and we continue to consult objective truth regarding all areas we're interested in. It's still always up to our own free volition to accept what objective truth has to say about this subject or that aspect, theme or topic, therefore there are no strings attached—it's absolute freedom.

OBJECTIVE TRUTH IN ACTION

Once we discover objective truth we'll treasure it, because it is not just plain information about something. There is a certain vitality to it and it is vibrant and in motion with unlimited power and energy to transform our lives and to take care of all problems that we encounter. It's not a head trip either; it's so simple that anyone with whatever size of intellectual capacity can understand it, grasp it, apply it and is invited to give it a try.

The precious United States of America, as the only nation in recent history, was founded on objective truth. By the application of objective truth by our forefathers as a heritage, America has enjoyed tremendous prosperity in every aspect of life in such a short period of time for so many years.

Objective truth produces certain characteristics in our life and these things are extremely important for each person. In fact, most people try to get these things and virtues through all kinds of efforts and self-help programs. In the end these programs will always fall short of obtaining these things in full measure with genuineness. Participants are left discouraged, having wasted a lot of time, soul power and physical energy. But objective truth will produce these much desired characteristics and effects automatically in every person that is willing to let objective truth do its work.

Occasionally we may need physical surgery after an accident or whatever, but rarely ever are we willing to have surgery done on our soul. All we need to do is to make a choice in hearing objective truth and consequently in accepting it. Objective truth will help us to make the first step. Objective truth will also kindly motivate us to make proper and beneficial decisions.

The benefits of the workings of objective truth are numerous. Relaxation, too, is a result of the workings of objective truth in us. The communication of objective truth will always produce an effect and provide powerful results. Objective truth is not just a compilation of letters, words and sentences printed on a page, but objective truth "is alive and full of power [making it active, operative, energizing, and effective]; it is sharper than any two-edged sword, penetrating to the dividing line of the breath of life (soul) and [the immortal] spirit, and of joints and marrow [of the deepest parts of our nature], exposing and sifting and analyzing and judging the very thoughts and purposes of the heart."[1] This is loaded and powerful stuff.

1   Hebrews 4:12, The Amplified Bible

DISCOVERING OBJECTIVE TRUTH

The written form of objective truth is called "Logos." It can be printed and read, and the Logos already produces a tremendous impact upon a person's life. Many religions have taken parts from the Logos and occasionally have included bits and pieces in their own philosophies. The written form of objective truth, if only bits and pieces are taken from it, does not represent the whole body of truth regarding a certain subject matter or an area in question. Never would such an approach cover or bring understanding to the entirety and whole spectrum of objective truth which is revealed.

There is a very important aspect to objective truth besides the Logos. In the Greek language this vital aspect is called "Rhema" which is nothing short of the Logos or the written form of objective truth made alive. That's when objective truth really hits home and things happen. A Rhema could be called a type of enlightenment. While other philosophies that are not based on objective truth or only take bits and pieces from objective truth may produce intellectual stimulation and definition creating some sort of excitement, only objective truth has the potential of the written word to be made alive. Plain intellectual knowledge doesn't produce life even though it may clear up certain things and explain various sophisticated details of life. To become effective, plain knowledge alone is dependent on the action of the recipient. Not so in the case of objective truth which once received by an individual is not necessarily dependent on the action of the recipient, but can become an active life-changing power with momentum by itself. Instead of just being a natural force producing mere natural results, objective truth, especially when the Rhema enters, becomes a supernatural spiritual force.

We must define objective truth and we must discover where objective truth can be found, because objective truth is the only permanent cure for depression. Why? As we already explained, depression starts in the mind and is most likely of supernatural origin, especially in the progression of its advanced stages. We can never cure the supernatural problem with natural means. Trying to cure depression with pills and medication will only provide a superficial temporary relief, but will never deal with the root problem. In an advanced stage of depression we may be sent to a psychiatrist which in turn will put us on medication trying to correct our chemical imbalance at least temporarily. This is just one more natural approach to healing a supernatural infection.

Before this advanced stage we may have to visit a psychologist or counselor on a weekly basis for a lengthy period of time. In each session we'll talk and he is possibly trying to help us to find and discover the root of our problems. Then we find a pseudo-solution and try it, but eventually it doesn't work and we're back at the psychologist's office. Psychological therapists are trained to listen to our problems in order to discover the possible cause of a certain problem. But by going through the past, which is their normal procedure, we dig up things that we don't need to dig up, because these things are already dead and buried. By focusing on these problems and by talking about them and by searching for causes of such problems, all these problems are being exalted, exaggerated and are emphasized, and in effect are given more strength if you will. Modern psychology believes that a patient has to speak out about what really bothers and hurts him or her. Instead of reacting to the world around us, we should share our frustrations with the therapist. By doing so these problems are just being magnified and eventually will grow to become even more difficult problems, even though for the moment there might be some relief, because the certain thing has been finally uttered and we don't need to keep it inside anymore. Just by talking about something without receiving precise wisdom or effective counsel that can truly help us, this will not provide a solution to a specific problem.

Many psychologists are able to analyze thought processes and how the mind and the emotions work, etc., but are unable to provide a cure or a solution that may bring genuine healing. Objective truth is rarely accepted or applied, because they do not consider it scientific enough and most of them haven't been trained in objective truth themselves. Aside from objective truth, operating in the best of their intentions and offering the best solutions they can offer, these solutions will always have limitations and will only be knowledge without power or life to change or solve any problems. This process leaves the patient virtually hopeless asking him or her to come back week after week in codependency. The patient is left running around frustrated with unresolved conflicts which are never really dealt with.

As things progress patients are directed by their therapist to see the psychiatrist and then—most likely—the patient has to endure a medical treatment consisting of drugs. Valuable years are being wasted and people are not being helped at all. The problems get worse and some commit suicide in the process, and others are left devastated in the end. Conventional psychology may even detect the root problem, but is unable to treat it effectively, because they're often not aware of the cure. So, these professionals try very hard to do their best, but they fall short of the supernatural provision and healing power of deliverance which only objective truth can furnish.

I once knew a psychiatrist who was well off financially and was the head doctor of a major mental institution. He was a very intelligent and respectable professional. While he lived in a very nice house, for years he wasn't willing to buy an automobile. So he had an old bicycle which he used to get to work every day. Through heavy traffic, even on rainy days he pedaled several miles to go to work and to come back home. At home he had piles of oriental rugs—one rug stacked over the other worth a small fortune. Some rooms were filled just with these piles of valuable oriental rugs. Finally, he gave in and after many years he bought a small old car for under a thousand dollars or so. I won't analyze his behavior, because he truly was a nice gentleman and one of the top psychiatrists in the country.

Another example in the late seventies was a thirty-five year old friend of mine who was a psychologist with his own practice. He opened his practice only twice a week for several hours. Since he was a compulsive gambler he spent most of his afternoons and evenings at a casino. Living in a small, but luxurious apartment and driving a Porsche, he surrounded himself with young girls barely eighteen years old. He was the confessed black sheep of his wealthy family. Nevertheless, he was a psychologist and he had been counseling hundreds of individuals. I won't analyze this case either, but my question to every patient would be, "Who is counseling you?" Meaning, while there are definitely many good professionals out there, still, many have their own problems and without objective truth they have a very hard time to get their own life in order. How are they supposed to provide quality counsel that can really help anyone?

We know of popular relationship counselors who have written bestselling books, conducted seminars, and taught their philosophies and findings on national television and on talk-radio seemingly being qualified to help people in need. But then we find out that they've been married three, four or even five times—not because their former wives or husbands died, but because of one divorce after the other. If you've been divorced, please don't feel or get condemned now, because it's not an issue. In some cases, as discussed in a previous chapter, a divorce is simply inevitable, because of some very serious reasons, etc. Divorced people have the same potential for a brand new beginning and an excellent marriage just like single people have, which have never been married before. And maybe you're already married again and your new marriage is just phenomenal—I really hope it is and I wish you the very best for it, truly.

Obviously, we already mentioned that nobody is perfect and certainly nobody has to be perfect, but it's also not too much to ask of those "professionals" (relationship counselors, psychologists, etc.) for some proof and evidence that their philosophy, advice and counsel really works. It should work at least to some degree in their own personal lives. For example, look at a workout video and check out the bodies of those fitness trainers, who usually have nicely shaped bodies. Rarely ever do you see an overweight 300-pound lady as a fitness trainer on such a show, because the shape of her body would be lacking evidence that her workout, philosophy and nutritional concept, etc. is really effective—there wouldn't be any visible evidence of it.

I'll always look at the real-life example of people that say this and that, because their personal life will testify to whether what they're saying is true or not and if this or that concept really works. It also tells us if they themselves actually believe what they teach and preach, or if they're just another phony. Of course, understanding, that these professionals, too, are just human and also make mistakes, and make wrong choices like we do and aren't perfect.

Everyone must go to the root of the problem and is in need to discover objective truth, so that we have a real chance to be healed from depression. Objective truth provides us with proven counsel and actual life-changing power to take care of our problems. We don't have to put much effort into it. All we need to do is to find objective truth and listen do it. The hearing of objective truth and its principles will bring cleansing and healing to the soul. As mentioned before, individuals may disagree with objective truth, because the extensive and consistent indoctrination of subjectivity has distorted our value system and our frame of reference—and we're left confused. Nevertheless, objective truth can definitely get our soul back in order. "The entrance and unfolding of Your words give light; their unfolding gives understanding (discernment and comprehension) to the simple."[1]

1   Psalm 119:130, The Amplified Bible

ACCEPTING OBJECTIVE TRUTH

In our day and age, especially in the civilized world, objective truth is easy to find, at least in its printed form. You can find a copy of objective truth in almost every bookstore.

To make a decision to hear objective truth is your part. Objective truth will motivate you to accept its wisdom and counsel, but still, it will always remain to be your personal decision to accept it for your own life.

As miraculous as the functions of the body and the mind of human beings are, mankind is intrinsically, basically and when left to himself, in a lost and desolate state, very arrogant and rebellious. To aid this depraved state of mankind we grow up in a deceptive world and are influenced day and night by things that do not stem from objective truth and that actually oppose objective truth. Therefore, individuals will frequently reject objective truth before they even give it a chance to prove itself at least a little bit. Instead, people go on the search and follow all kinds of weird philosophies and ideas, but rarely ever do they give objective truth a chance.

Being raised a Roman Catholic, as a teenager I wasn't convinced that Christianity the way it was presented to me in Catholicism was really the right religion. I was an altar boy and we were taught religion week after week in the public schools. A few things that bothered me especially and just didn't feel right in Catholicism were for instance, that the priests couldn't get married, that I had to confess my sins to a man and that I seemingly couldn't confess my sins to God alone, the cultic Mary stuff, the purgatory, and that there wasn't any life there, but only dead religious formalities. I must say that I do appreciate the kindness we received and also several things that we were taught there. For many years I've searched and studied one thing after the other—psychology, various religions, all kinds of human philosophies and concepts, etc. At one point in my life Buddhism was an interesting consideration. Fact is, that there is a lot of stuff out there. Some theories or philosophies may be more appealing or interesting to one person than to another.

Throughout the years I've learned and have come to the conclusion that there are in fact only two religions or systems of thought/belief available to mankind. One religion is based on what a person can do by their own efforts and in their own strength for God, whoever and whatever their god might be, in order to please this god or to be accepted by their god. And the other system of thought/belief is based on what God has already done for mankind, and that He has made everything already available to every man and woman as a free gift, simply by accepting/receiving it as such, without the pressure of a person's self-effort or reliability on personal strength of an individual. If you would be able to study every religious philosophy you would end up with the same conclusion that only these two systems of thought/belief or religion exist. One is self-centered by trying to please God by our own efforts and merits, and this certain religion is widespread throughout the world, but it's only a religious system leaving mankind to their own ability of performance by their own limited strength and intellectual capacity. This type of religion is found with virtually all religious systems including Christianity.

Only pure Christianity offers the opportunity to accept the other system of thought which is the religion of absolute freedom in which God has already done everything to appease His justice and to provide mankind the opportunity to freely accept His plan of deliverance and salvation on a personal basis. Therefore man can be restored to a close-knit relationship and even fellowship with the Creator, without being under the pressure, stress, bondage and fear of trying to please a perfect God by his own imperfect efforts. The guilt is removed, too.

When we come to the pure source of objective truth we should come there without religious prejudice, and without preconceived ideas. This liberty and deliverance is offered by God Himself and is fully explained in His Word, the Bible. In the Bible, which is the complete and accurate Word of God revealed to mankind in it's written form, objective truth in its entirety is revealed. Remember, it's first the written word, but as we hear and accept objective truth it becomes the Living Word. The Bible is still the number one bestseller in the world year after year—there must be a very good reason for it. While the Word of God is unchangeable and is always the same, the teachings of the Bible have been misrepresented and distorted by self-centered men over and over again. Still, it doesn't change the fact that the Word of God continues to be absolutely true as the only source for objective truth. The Bible hasn't changed a bit, it's still the Good Book, fully inspired by God Himself. The Bible contains everything that God wanted to communicate and share with mankind.

Will you give objective truth a chance, or will you reject it? It's a choice that you personally have to make. It is for certain that objective truth doesn't want to hurt you, but instead wants to bring healing and deliverance as mentioned in the introductory verse of this book. Psalm 107:20 (KJV) states that "He sent His word and healed them, and delivered them from their destructions." If we give objective truth a chance to speak to us so that we may hear it, we immediately give God a chance to let Him make His word alive to us. His word will shed light on every important subject and theme regarding life, death and God, and it will bring understanding. Most importantly, God's Word will heal our soul and deliver us from our destructions, also securing effectively our eternal destiny.

Accepting objective truth doesn't mean you'll become a Jesus-freak, or a religious fanatic, or that you accept another limited format of some religious box or system of "Dos" and "Don'ts." Instead we'll show you how the practical application of the Word of God will certainly eliminate depression in your life and how easy it is to build a protective wall of truth avoiding depression altogether. The Word of God is actually the mind of

God, meaning what God Himself thinks about every topic. That's not a bad mind to have, because the major attributes of God are omnipresence, omniscience, omnipotence and immutability. Also, God doesn't lie and cannot lie and He doesn't change His mind either. Objective truth, namely His Word, is absolutely accurate and without error and we can trust it without reservation. Its very nature and wisdom are rooted in all of God's attributes and His character—it's His mind.

In the process of applying the Word of God in various areas of our lives it will also eliminate guilt, anxiety and stress, producing true substance and purpose in our life. You'll save a lot of money on medication and counseling sessions, because the need for them will cease.

By this decision to hear the Word of God you will effectively help yourself and also the loved ones and people around you. The Word of God will always have an effect and produce eternal results.

5

MORE THAN CONQUERORS

Most people live a defeated life. By their appearance with the presentation of their material possessions or by the things they say and do they try to make an impression to look like winners. "Look at my golden Rolex and look at my new Ferrari," they say. While these things are enjoyable to some degree and may indicate that, according to the temporal value system, these individuals have seemingly made it, the accumulation of money or possessions does not testify of these people being true winners inside their soul. People have killed themselves by having too much and they became bored because they seemingly couldn't find another materialistic challenge to conquer. In the pursuit of money and wealth, which ultimately should have bought them and their loved ones some comfort and happiness, they frequently forget to take care of their own spiritual health and inner being and the spiritual health of their loved ones. "For what shall it profit a man, if he shall gain the whole world, and lose his own soul?"[1]

Imagine becoming more than conquerors independent and apart from outward circumstances and possessions. Each person has the opportunity to obtain so much freedom and victory inside his soul that at times it seems almost too much to cope with, which of course, it isn't, but it's all just so overwhelming. No matter what happens, there can be tremendous peace in your soul and nothing can upset you anymore. Clear thinking at all times has many benefits. A sound mind stabilizes the emotions and the nervous system. All of a sudden, hostile reactions will no longer be part of your life. Nasty and stupid comments by some jerk will not set us off anymore. Instead, we stand secure on a solid foundation that is unshakable.

1   Mark 8:36, KJV

HEALING OF THE SOUL

To fill the mind with God's thinking will heal the entire soul with its thought process and the response system. How do we fill our mind with God's thinking? First of all, it's not a system of self-effort, but rather a choice of making yourself available to hear the Word of God on a consistent basis. God's amazing grace will not only do the rest, but will virtually do everything.

If you like to know what the Word of God says about a certain subject you may go to the concordance in the back portion of your Bible. Look up a certain word or theme and you'll find several verses in which this word or topic is mentioned. If you like to study a specific subject more extensively a Study Bible, e.g. The Thompson Chain-Reference® Bible, will be of tremendous help. Studying the Bible in specific categories will provide you with the exact mind of God in particular areas and in regard to specific themes and subjects. It will let you know what God thinks about it and what the objective truth is pertaining to such a particular topic.

Of course, it will be very beneficial to hang around people that are interested in the same thing and may even believe the same things you do. Therefore a Bible-believing church will be a great asset in the life of every person. It basically doesn't matter with what denomination, if any, this certain local church is affiliated with, as long as it's a Bible-believing church that preaches and teaches the Word of God. At the local church you'll find spiritual shelter, but also encouragement and probably true friends that will accept you just the way you are. Whoever you are, and whatever your habits may be, they will accept you just as you are. It's not that easy anymore to find a true Bible-believing church. Yes, many may say that they believe this and that, but what is the key to finding out if it's the real thing? We've already mentioned, that it is the Word of God made alive. Meaning, while the Logos can be very beneficial and helpful, you must receive a personal Rhema to really believe the Word of God for practical application in your life. You will receive a Rhema in a local church where the pastor is anointed. There is another word "Anointing" or "anointed" that may be foreign to you. But an "Anointing" regarding a pastor of a local church can be explained as a pastor who has received a personal Rhema about the written Word himself. When he preaches and teaches, the message is loaded and powerful—it's real and it is like God speaking Himself, using a frail human being as a vessel to communicate His Word. You know when you hear it that this is the real thing.

The pure communication of the Word of God will heal your soul automatically. All a person can really do is to make a positive choice to listen to the Word of God and when hearing it to accept it, effectively agreeing with it and letting the Word of God do the work in the individual. Practical applications of the Word of God in practical life situations will follow and the Word of God will become resident in the soul—cleansing and healing the soul. It's not that difficult.

In fact, there is one more vital and the most important aspect to understanding objective truth and to letting the Word of God come into a person for healing the soul. The Son of God, Jesus Christ, came to earth in the form of a human being, about two thousand years ago. He came for a distinctive purpose. Jesus Christ was not a prophet like many religions teach, but He was indeed the Son of God. Originally, the human race rebelled against God and in our natural being while we have a need for God we're not really looking for God nor are we eager to find God. This rebellion is called sin and separation from God was and is the result. Therefore every man and woman must be reconciled to God, but we're unable to reconcile ourselves to God in our own natural strength. Many religious groups and organizations try very hard to do so, but it's simply impossible. How can an imperfect human being fulfill the perfect justice of a perfect God? He can't, only God can do it for us and provide a way or means of reconciliation. Every person is in need of the Savior.

There is an empty place in all of us and this place is reserved for Jesus Christ, God Himself. Man is unable to reconcile himself to God, but there is no need for man to do this, because Jesus Christ has already done it. Jesus Christ died on the cross of Calvary and paid the penalty for all sins of the world. Jesus Christ was absolutely sinless and by the choice of His free will, motivated by God's unconditional love, and as the only qualified person that ever lived to do so, He took upon Himself all sins of the human race. He accepted the sentence and penalty for all sins of humanity from the past, present and future, so that we as frail and sinful human beings only need to believe that He did this for us. He has done this for us because of His unconditional and limitless love. As we hear the Word of God we are able to believe that Jesus Christ is truly our Savior. We make a decision to trust Jesus Christ for what He did for us on that certain cross of Calvary. As we look to Jesus for our salvation from the penalty of sin, trusting in Him as our Savior, in this very moment many beautiful things happen.

Jesus Christ not only died for all the sins of the world on the cross of Calvary, but on the third day He rose from the dead, which makes it possible for us to receive Eternal Life at the very moment we believe and trust in Jesus Christ as our Savior. Because He rose from the dead this Eternal Life is full of supernatural resurrection life power of divine origin. At this very moment of believing in Him we also receive the Holy Spirit that dwells from then on in us until we die in our physical body. Not some day in the future, but at the very moment of salvation a person receives Eternal Life. Meaning, no matter what may happen in our life on earth in the future, after we've once received Eternal Life we have a definite and unchangeable guarantee to be in the presence of God for all eternity.

Salvation is the work of God and it doesn't depend on our efforts, it's free—a free gift we only need to accept it. We don't have to change first, or do anything else, but just come to Him as we are. No matter how guilty and

unworthy we feel, or what our lifestyle might be, or
what sins we may continuously commit—it doesn't
matter, He wants us to receive the free gift of salvation
right now, because He prepared this free gift of Eternal
Life for every single person. Jesus Christ said about
Himself, "I am the way, the truth, and the life: no man
cometh unto the Father, but by me."[1] "For God so loved
the world, that He gave His only begotten Son, that
whoever believes in Him should not perish, but have
eternal life."[2] "He who believes in the Son has eternal
life."[3] "Believe on the Lord Jesus Christ, and thou shalt
be saved."[4] "For by grace are ye saved through faith; and
that not of yourselves: it is the gift of God."[5]

It's a personal decision each person must make
personally as an individual. Think of it as someone who
has a gift for you and reaches out to you to give you this
gift. This someone doesn't put any demands on you, nor
does this someone have any expectations of you, but he
just simply wants to give you the gift. It's up to us to
make a free volitional choice to take the gift in order to
possess it. Once we've taken the gift it's ours and we
benefit from the gift. As long as we don't accept the gift
we won't benefit from the gift. But all we have to do is
simply accept the gift. The acceptance of the gift is
unconditional.

How can you accept this gift of salvation and therefore receive Eternal Life right now? If it makes sense to
you that Jesus Christ is the only One that can bridge the
gap between man and God—if you simply believe this in
your heart, please pray a simple prayer like this:

"Dear Lord Jesus, I know I'm a sinner
and I cannot save myself. I believe that
You have died for me and that You have
paid in full for all of my sins. Come into
my heart to live as I gladly accept You
as my personal Lord and Savior
right now. Thank you."

If you've prayed a prayer like this and truly meant
it in your heart, you are now saved forever and Christ
lives in you through the Holy Spirit, leading and guiding
you in your life as you let Him. Your eternal destiny is
secure and you've received Eternal Life. Take a cal-
ender and mark today's date on it as your spiritual
birthday—it's true and no matter what anybody will
ever say to you, it cannot be changed ever again,
because today you've received Jesus Christ as your
personal Savior and this is your spiritual birthday.

As we accept salvation the Holy Spirit takes residence in us instantly. Because the Holy Spirit dwells in
us we will begin to understand the Word of God and
therefore receive a Rhema. The written Word will all of
a sudden have personal power in our life. In Romans
1:16 (KJV) we read that this Good News, the Gospel of
Jesus Christ, "Is the power of God unto salvation to
every one that believeth." The Word of God is powerful.
The Word of God is the power unto salvation, meaning
it is the power that will lead us gently to the point of
accepting Jesus Christ as Savior, and it is available to

us to heal us and to deliver us from our destructions.

What did we do to receive healing in our soul? Virtually nothing. We were just motivated to make a positive decision to hear the Word of God and once we've heard it we were motivated to agree with the Word of God. The Word does the work through the Holy Spirit in us. God consists of three persons that are one and these three persons are the Father, the Son and the Holy Spirit. These three are God. Therefore God does the work in us, because the Holy Spirit is one person of the triune God. It can't be any easier than that and anybody can receive a healing in their soul by simply making a choice of hearing the Word of God. We can step in front of a perfect God just the way we are. We don't need to change, because in ourselves we're unable to really produce a perfect change. Your current habitual sins or lifestyle, etc. are not the issue, He just wants you to come to Him just as you are, accepting Jesus Christ as your personal Savior.

When you go to a doctor the doctor doesn't expect you to heal yourself. You're going to the doctor just as sick as you are, because you expect him to heal you. This is just another example to illustrate that God is simply asking you to come to Him just as you are, and the healing will take place as you come to Him. You can expect God to heal you. "Christ in you, the hope of glory."6 Meaning when you accept Jesus Christ as your personal Lord and Savior, at this very moment Christ will begin the healing process in you. It's Christ who does the work in you and you can expect Him to produce a change and healing as necessary. "For it is God who is at work in you."[7]

1   John 14:6, KJV
2   John 3:16, NASB
3   John 3:36, NASB
4   Acts 16:31, KJV
5   Ephesians 2:8, KJV
6   Colossians 1:27, KJV
7   Philippians 2:13, NASB

CONQUER THE IMPOSSIBLE

We have another word that we must address, in order to understand it properly when it's used in this book. The word is "Faith." In it's true meaning "Faith" is a relentless trust in Jesus Christ, or a dependence on God despite all outward circumstances. Contrary to popular belief, this faith cannot be produced by the efforts of human beings. At conception in the womb, every single person receives a measure of faith by God. It's up to every individual once born into this world and in the process of growing up, to use this certain initial measure of faith to direct it towards God and reap divine benefits with everlasting results, or to use this initial faith otherwise to pursue something else.

Once again, pure and genuine faith is a supernatural production and man is only the recipient of such faith. Mankind is not the producer of genuine faith, but instead God is the producer and giver of faith. Aside from the initial measure of faith, every other portion of faith for specific situations or for understanding particular segments of the Word of God comes by hearing the Word of God. Faith is imparted as we hear the Word of God. This is phenomenal. All we do is simply make a choice to listen to the Word of God and supernatural faith is imparted to us. If you've just accepted Jesus Christ as your personal Savior then this principle can be illustrated in that you've heard the Word of God and therefore faith was imparted to you. As you exercised your free volition positively in agreeing with the Word of God, it effectively resulted in you trusting in Jesus Christ for your salvation. The more we hear the Word of God the easier it will be to trust Jesus Christ also in various life situations and for revelations described and taught in the Bible.

One principle taught in the Bible regarding conquering the impossible is shown when Jesus said, "I say to you, if you have faith as a mustard seed, you shall say to this mountain, 'Move from here to there,' and it shall move; and nothing shall be impossible to you."[1] "For with God nothing shall be impossible."[2] Faith is a gift from God. As we hear the Word of God we receive faith. Amazingly, not the quantity of faith is an issue, because any portion of faith provided by God is of divine origin. Even faith the size of a mustard seed, which is pretty much the smallest seed in existence, can literally move mountains because of its supernatural origin and quality. As we trust God, even with only the faith the size of a mustard seed, it is His performance and work to actually move the mountain, and we simply trust Him to do it and we're standing by watching Him with expectations based on His character to do it. The mountain may consist of seemingly unsurpassable problems within the scope and view of our own limited natural strength. These problems may be in whatever area— maybe regarding relationships, health, finances, a bad temper, depression, alcohol, drugs, or whatever, but God can move the mountain when we simply exercise faith as we trust in Him.

Meaning we learn to trust God with all of our heart for all kinds of situations. When we accepted Christ we trusted Him for the eternal destiny of our soul and now we can trust Him for the details of life. As just mentioned, not the quantity of faith is the issue, but rather the quality of faith is important. People have natural faith and they use it improperly directed for their own achievements and desires. But when God's faith is applied by a person things really get in motion and the impossible becomes possible. No longer is it the energy and self-effort of an individual, but instead it is God Almighty who is moving with the full energy and power of His kingdom on our behalf.

This is simply phenomenal, because it excludes the frustrating efforts and limited actions by human beings, and freely gives God a way to demonstrate His unlimited power, love and grace to mankind. Is there a problem in your life? No problem is too big for God and

He can take care of everything, because He truly cares for us. "Casting the whole of your care [all your anxieties, all your worries, all your concerns, once and for all] on Him, for He cares for you affectionately and cares about you watchfully."3 "Do not fret or have any anxiety about anything, but in every circumstance and in everything, by prayer and petition (definite requests), with thanksgiving, continue to make your wants known to God."4 "I can do all things through Christ which strengtheneth me."5 Instead of going to a session with a counselor we simply go to God in prayer. Prayer is talking with God, and letting Him know whatever bothers us. We tell Him about things we simply don't understand and we ask Him to take care of our problems. Approaching problems in such a manner will not exalt a problem and therefore negativity is not able to creep in, but by exercising faith as we rely on God to answer our prayers and by trusting in Him for our worries and problems, we'll see God in action. Remember, when talking with Him, give Him a chance to speak to you, too. It won't be a loud audible voice, but it's going to be the still small voice of 1 Kings 19:12.

The Bible contains over seven thousand promises available to the believer. All these promises are yours. Can you imagine this? There are a few things God cannot do and one of those things is that He cannot lie, meaning all his promises are true and He will keep and fulfill each one of His promises no matter what. Isn't this wonderful? All of a sudden you found Someone whom you can trust without reservation and who will not lie to you. While we may not be able to see God at this time, we can certainly see His works and the results of His actions. Can you imagine praying to an invisible God and telling Him your wishes and the desires of your heart, and suddenly your prayers are answered specifically. The answer to your prayers has visible results. This is also evidence that God is real and that everything He said is true.

Some people may suffer from physical problems, maybe it's cancer, maybe it's something minor, or whatever, but God is certainly able to heal you even in a moment of time. Most certainly He'll give you peace for the situation immediately. Maybe you have relationship problems of whatever kind, and once again God is able to move with His Holy Spirit to bring restoration and healing to these situations. Maybe there are financial problems and it's seemingly a hopeless situation, but God can come through and provide a tremendous financial reversal. Or, maybe it's drug abuse or alcohol that plagues you day in and day out and you're seemingly helpless to get rid of it, but God can come through miraculously and deliver you without much hassle. As you hear the Word of God on a continuous basis you'll be in awe of what God can and will do in your life and the lives of other believers.

While we won't get angry at God if He doesn't take care of certain problems or situations immediately, we can definitely expect God to do the impossible, because that's what He does. I've seen it myself so many times, physical healing, financial blessings, marriages restored supernaturally, and people being delivered from all kinds of bad habits, e.g. drug addiction, alcoholism, sexual perversions, etc. and it all happened, sometimes in an instant and sometimes it took a little while. People are being delivered and healed from depressions and are truly set free from the bondage and slavery of depressive moods and their devastating effects. It certainly isn't your willpower, but it may depend on your will to be exercised positively towards simply hearing the Word of God, but there is absolutely no effort on your part to be more than a conqueror and to conquer the impossible. Even regarding your free will it is phenomenal that God will lovingly motivate you to exercise your free will positively towards Him, but of course, He can't force Himself upon you, because you're an individual made in the image of God and you have a free will.

To conquer the impossible and to receive all the blessings prepared for you simply listen to the Word of God taught by a true man of God and things will work out just fine. We, as the children of God have a great promise, "We know that God causes all things to work together for good."[6]

1   Matthew 17:20, NASB
2   Luke 1:37, KJV
3   1 Peter 5:7, The Amplified Bible
4   Philippians 4:6, The Amplified Bible
5   Philippians 4:13, KJV
6   Romans 8:28, NASB

6

A PERFECT LIFE
ABUNDANT LIFE

I s there such a thing as a perfect life here on earth? In this book we could have used solely a psychological approach, but it would not have helped you, because it would have left you once again to yourself and your own efforts in your natural strength. To use just a psychological approach would not have been an honest effort on my part, because of what I personally believe in and because of what I've seen studying human behavior in over two decades.

Any kind of psychological analysis and quality program must include and deal with spiritual issues. There are many books out there that have solely a psychological approach, and there are also many books out there that have solely a spiritual approach. A book with only a spiritual approach may not be understood by people that are not familiar with spiritual issues, and therefore such a book may not produce the answers, solutions and results expected by the reader with none or only limited spiritual capacity. It doesn't mean that these books are bad, or whatever, and in fact many of these books are probably very helpful and provide tremendous insight. But rarely ever do you find a book like this one, the one you're reading right now that carefully has utilized a unique blend of a psychological and spiritual approach. We've tried to reach out to every person in whatever state of mind, etc. they may be and whatever size capacity they may have.

Solely psychological books will always focus on our limited human capacity. It's only in the spiritual realm that we can enter into a world of divine proportions. Every human being is a trichotomy, which means that every person consists of three basic parts, namely the physical body, the soul and the human spirit. The spirit cannot be seen, but it's the spirit that should control the soul. At the very moment of salvation, meaning when a person makes a decision to accept Jesus Christ as their personal Savior, the Holy Spirit comes in and energizes the human spirit. That's why such a person is called a born-again Christian, because at such a point in life, at the very moment of salvation, a person is born of the Spirit of God and it's his spiritual birthday.

As we study the Word of God and let the Holy Spirit minister unto us in making the Word of God alive to us, that's when the human spirit is enabled to control the human soul with the mind of God. In this process the soul will be continuously cleansed and healed, and even as the soul is invisible we're literally able to experience a healthy soul and eventually will see the effects of a healthy soul.

While the physical body must die once sooner or later and is only temporal, the spiritual being of man is immortal. To further clarify some religious concepts various groups may have, there is no such thing as a reincarnation. Objective truth explains that "It is appointed unto men once to die, but after this the judgment."[1] This fact settles the issue in a hurry and eliminates speculations regarding this topic that would otherwise only confuse a person. For a born-again Christian it means that to be absent from the body is to be present with the Lord. When a Christian dies physically, his spiritual being is immediately in the presence of God. Isn't that a comforting promise? Well, it's absolutely true and leaves no room for speculations as well takes away all the confusion of what happens after our body dies.

1   Hebrews 9:27, KJV

TRUE IDENTITY

In the beginning of this book we've discussed the identity crisis, which almost every person will go through, and which will lead them most likely sooner or later into depression. Once we find our true identity things will change tremendously as security, certainty, assurance and confidence will be imparted to us by the Holy Spirit as we hear the Word of God.

Objective truth will also explain to us and supply us with positional truth. Positional truth is simply what we are in the eyes of God, meaning how God sees us in Christ. Positional truth is based on objective truth and cannot be changed as it is an eternal fact. Our daily experience as human beings is called experiential truth, meaning things that really happen in our experience day by day. If we focus on positional truth then experiential truth won't be able to defeat us. A focus on experiential truth more likely than not will lead us into depression, because our true identity based on positional truth is often not realized in experiential truth. How do we focus on positional truth? As we study and hear the Word of God our concentration is on things above so to speak, or on positional facts, which are positional truth. Details and circumstances of mundane life are readily able to distract us and to take away our concentration and focus from things above.

That's why it's so important to let the Word of God in every category become resident in our soul. Then, at the moment of attack, the Holy Spirit is able to bring to remembrance the objective Word of God to defeat any onslaught of subjectivity. When subjectivity doesn't find entrance to our minds, our souls won't be affected negatively to produce reactions. Instead we're able to reign in objectivity to respond with healthy emotions. This is not a self-help program based on our own efforts, but as mentioned before, the power of God through the Holy Spirit does the work for us and in us. Even as the Holy Spirit and the Word of God will motivate us to make a positive choice to accept objective truth, because of our free volition it will always remain our decision to let the Holy Spirit do His work. To accept and agree with the Word of God and the process of letting the Holy Spirit do His work in us is called to be filled with the Holy Spirit, because He is able to work in us freely to His full extent without being hindered by our egotistical self or by subjectivity.

What does positional truth say about our real state of being in Christ? Or what does positional truth say about our heavenly position of who we are and what we've become since we've accepted Jesus Christ as Savior? First of all it says that "If any man be in Christ, he is a new creature: old things are passed away; behold, all things are become new."[1] Well, in our experience it is not necessarily so, even though some old things may have already gone away and some other things may have become new.

Example for experiential application: If you once were a drug addict, but you're not a drug addict now, you are no longer a drug addict. There are certain counseling and self-help programs that tell you to confess that if you were an alcoholic twenty years ago, you're supposed to continue to say that you're still an alcoholic today. It's one thing to acknowledge certain habits back then when these things were a problem in order to confess sin as such and this, of course, is proper, but it's another thing to consistently focus on old habits once they've been dealt with and are no longer an issue. If the focus is on consistent acknowledgment of these old habits which have already been done away with, then there is a consistent danger of reviving these old habits, because they stay fresh in the memory. If we're consistently reminded of these old things, eventually in a moment of weakness we will fall back to these old habits.

Once alcoholism or drug addiction, or any other habit or perverted lifestyle have been dealt with and have been done away with, you're no longer an alcoholic or addict, etc. It would be a lie to say otherwise. In fact, you've only been an alcoholic for a certain period in your life. If you've been clean for a certain amount of time, then you're no longer an alcoholic. Your identity should be an absolutely new one and no one has the right to associate you of being an alcoholic. The past is not an issue anymore, because it's already gone. Don't let people lie to you and if they do ignore them and avoid them. Anytime someone brings up the past or negative things from the past, it's time to say "Good-bye" to these people, because they're infectious and destructive.

To be a new creation in Christ means that in our

spiritual position all things have become new. No longer are we lost sinners, but now we are saved sinners who have Eternal Life which nobody can ever take away from us. Yes, we're still sinners and we fail and we make mistakes, but God looks at us as perfect individuals, because He sees Christ in us. God can only see Christ in us when we've accepted Christ once in our life as our Savior.

Our experience does not affect the status of our heavenly position. This heavenly status can no longer be changed, not even if we ourselves would like to change it for whatever reason. We are new creatures in Christ and that's how God looks at us forever. It is impossible to change God's view of us by our thoughts or things we say or do. Once Christ came into our heart that's where He's going to be and nothing can separate us ever from Christ again. No longer do we have to live in fear of uncertain death not knowing where we'll be when we die. We'll be with Jesus in absolute happiness forever. No longer do we have to be afraid of what people or circumstances can do to us in this life, because our eternal destiny is secure and we have judicial peace with God. Meaning God is judicially on our side, even though our experience, because of wrong choices and undefined rebellion in us, etc. may not necessarily compliment this view from our human viewpoint.

It's a good thing to have God on our side and He supports us with His Word and His Holy Spirit. As we learn to think with Him we'll be enabled to make right choices, which with confidence can be referred to as

God's perfect choices. It's fun to make the right decisions, because we'll also reap the blessings, rewards
and consequences of right choices, which are automatic
results. Don't you think it's fun to get your specific
prayers answered precisely? When we're in sync with
God a lot of great things happen.

At the very moment of salvation a person becomes
a child of God and this person also receives heavenly
citizenship, which is permanent. There are no deporta-
tion procedures available in the Kingdom of Heaven—
once a citizen of Heaven, you'll always be a citizen of
Heaven. We also receive diplomatic status by becoming
ambassadors for Christ at the very moment of salvation
and hopefully we'll apply this positional fact also to our
experience. We're a chosen generation, a royal priest-
hood, a holy nation and a peculiar people. Your divine
position elevates you into royalty in a blink of an eye and
provides you with diplomatic status. This is what's true
about you. This is your true identity. While you're still
on earth you're heavenly royalty and you carry diplomatic status as an ambassador for Jesus Christ. It's
real. It's a fact and we can even experience our position
as long as we continue to walk the earth.

Maybe someone says to you that you're no good, and
maybe your lifestyle doesn't reflect your divine position.
Nevertheless, your true identity doesn't change by what
people say, or by what you do, or by how you feel. Your
divine position is secured. Take a moment, think about
it and dwell on it.

1   2 Corinthians 5:17, KJV

NEVER ALONE AGAIN

You're not alone, even if you don't have many or any friends on earth, you're not alone. I remember before I got hold of some basic truths about real Christianity I was sobbing for hours and even days, because loneliness encompassed me. With loneliness came self-pity and the down spiral to manic depressive behavior was in full motion.

Christians have the amazing opportunity to develop a personal relationship with Jesus Christ and are encouraged to pursue such a relationship. In the process of developing a real relationship and even fellowship with Jesus Christ, which could be defined as our vertical, the development of relationships with people around us will become a phenomenal experience, which could be defined as our horizontal.

Listen to what God has to say about what He most certainly will continuously do for us, "For He [God] Himself has said, I will not in any way fail you nor give you up nor leave you without support. [I will] not, [I will] not, [I will] not in any degree leave you helpless nor forsake nor let [you] down (relax My hold on you)! [Assuredly not!]."₁ "Whither shall I go from thy spirit? or whither shall I flee from thy presence? If I ascend up into heaven, thou art there: if I make my bed in hell, behold, thou art there. If I take the wings of the morning, and dwell in the uttermost parts of the sea; Even there shall thy hand lead me, and thy right hand shall hold me. If I say, Surely the darkness shall cover me; even the night shall be light about me."₂ "Can a woman forget her nursing child, And have no compassion on the son of her womb? Even these may forget, but I will not forget you. Behold, I have inscribed you on the palms of My hands."₃

Another great passage of assurance, confidence and comfort in the Bible can be found in Psalm 23 (KJV):

> "The Lord is my shepherd; I shall not
> want. He maketh me to lie down in
> green pastures: he leadeth me beside
> the still waters. He restoreth my soul:
> he leadeth me in the paths of righteousness
> for his name's sake. Yea, though I walk
> through the valley of the shadow of death,
> I will fear no evil: for thou art with me;
> thy rod and thy staff they comfort me.
> Thou preparest a table before me in the
> presence of mine enemies: thou anointest
> my head with oil; my cup runneth over.
> Surely goodness and mercy shall follow
> me all the days of my life: and I will dwell
> in the house of the Lord for ever."

Read this Psalm 23 word for word and listen to the still small voice of God massaging your soul. Whenever you feel like some depressive moods are about to sneak in, begin reading the Psalms slowly. Start with Psalm 1. Substitute the word "law" with "Word of God" because that's what it actually means anyway. When the Word of God finds entry into your heart, you should be back on your feet thinking and functioning in objectivity after several Psalms. Depending on the level of depression that has already creeped in, it may take sometimes up to thirty Psalms to be back on track. Nevertheless, it really works. I've seen people that were determined to commit suicide and had it already all planned how they would kill themselves within the next few hours. But by applying this method were turned away from their suicidal behavior and received tremendous hope and appreciation for life and are still alive today.

Seeds of suicide may be accumulated over the years and finally people snap and commit this unthinkable act. Usually the actual decision to commit the act of suicide happens in just a moment. Many suicidal candidates are deeply thankful when they're saved from their attempt. We must build protective walls in our soul so that seeds of suicide cannot be sown and enter. These destructive thoughts must be kept out. This can be effectively accomplished by thinking positively with God and having His mind imparted by making it resident in our soul. As we hear and study the Word of God this is accomplished by the Holy Spirit in us. In time of need the Holy Spirit is able to recall the Word of God to our consciousness, if the Word of God is stored up in our soul. Therefore it is crucial to hear the Word of God over and over again, and to study it in specific categories just like we do right now.

Single people may often think that it is only they who can be overcome with feelings of loneliness, but it happens to married people, too. Earlier in this book we discussed celebrities, people that are surrounded by multitudes of fans and staff, but they often will feel lonely and depression will creep in. If we're available to develop a close personal relationship with Jesus Christ, loneliness will not be able to drag us down, because we'll find comfort in Him, and the Word will be alive to provide clear thinking in crisis situations. "Draw near to God and He will draw near to you."4 We draw near to God when we attend church services, when we study His Word and in prayer communicate with Him, as we relentlessly trust in Him, because of who He is. His promises will encourage us and are definitely all ours.

It's when we realize our true identity in Christ and the love that God has demonstrated towards us in putting such a high value on each one of us by sacrificing His own Son for us, that we're finally able to love ourselves properly. He truly loves each one of us so much and you can see He truly cares for you and me. His love for you and me is the major reason you and I can say "I love me" to ourselves. As we've already discussed, it's not a selfish love, but we're simply in awe that the Almighty God Who made everything in the universe is concerned about each human being and loves each one of us so very much. When we realize His love for us in this way we'll be able to love ourselves properly and love others as we love ourselves.

1   Hebrews 13:5, The Amplified Bible
2   Psalm 139:7-11, KJV
3   Isaiah 49:15-16, NASB
4   James 4:8, NASB

CLEAR THINKING • CORRECT FOCUS

The precious Word of God encourages clear thinking in objectivity. Meaning we do not need to make decisions based on our feelings and preconceived distorted opinions which are based in subjectivity. Instead we can be very objective while healthy emotions will compliment our positive thoughts, choices and actions.

There will always come about some strange thoughts and attacks so to speak. "[Inasmuch as we] refute arguments and theories and reasonings and every proud and lofty thing that sets itself up against the [true] knowledge of God; and we lead every thought and purpose away captive into the obedience of Christ."[1]

The remedy for clear thinking to avoid depression and to experience a victorious life is clearly laid out in the Scriptures. "Whatever is true, whatever is honorable, whatever is right, whatever is pure, whatever is lovely, whatever is of good repute, if there is any excellence and if anything worthy of praise, let your mind dwell on these things."[2] To avoid the early beginnings of discouragement and the progression of depression "I will set no wicked thing before mine eyes."[3] The eyes and ears are the initial perceptive sources of communication. While the attacks themselves may not be avoidable, the effects of attacks on our mind can be altogether avoided effectively by not letting our eyes watch and our ears hear deceptive, subjective and destructive things.

As we dwell on the things of God and ponder His

Word, we're being transformed by the renewing of our mind and we're being renewed in the spirit of our mind. It's a complete renewal. What goes in must come out and if we have a continuous intake of the Word of God, only godly things will come out. Once again, we won't be perfect here on earth and we don't try to be perfect. We will still do things we actually don't want to do. But we will not be defeated by focusing on our imperfections, but instead we will enjoy the fruits of true success by focusing on Jesus Christ. Our failures are not the issue, but Jesus Christ is the issue.

The focus must always be on Christ. "Look to me, and be ye saved."[4] At the time of your salvation when you received Jesus Christ as your Savior, the focus was not on your sins or on what you could do for God, or on who you were at that time, or in what condition you were at that time, but the focus was on Jesus Christ. You had to trust solely in Him and nothing else. To look to Him means that without reservation we only look to Him and nothing else matters. That's how salvation is received.

In everyday life regarding all problems the same is true. It is illustrated in the Old Testament in Numbers, chapter twenty-one, when under the leadership of Moses the Israelites were led out of their captivity in Egypt into the wilderness. The Israelites complained that God was seemingly not providing enough food and water for them. "Then the Lord sent fiery (burning) serpents among the people; and they bit the people, and many Israelites died."[5] The historical record goes on to explain that after the deadly serpents killed many Israelites they repented (changed their mind) and were sorry for their complaining. They asked Moses to pray to God for a solution to their problem regarding the deadly serpents. Moses received specific instructions from God. "And Moses made a serpent of bronze and put it on a pole, and if a serpent had bitten any man, when he looked to the serpent of bronze [attentively, expectantly, with a steady and absorbing gaze], he lived."6

To look on the wounds and to deal or take care of the wounds themselves would not have healed anyone or kept any victims alive. It was the exercise of believing the Word of God and in trusting solely in the provision of God, which was for them to simply look to this serpent of bronze on a pole, that they were healed and survived. This serpent of bronze represents the power of Satan—the serpent—destroyed by Jesus Christ on the cross of Calvary. No longer did the poisonous serpents have any power to kill and to destroy the Israelites, but God's provision produced absolute healing and life. If we accept the provision of God our problems and wounds in the soul and depressions, etc. will have no longer any power to hurt us and to drag us down to destroy us, but instead through God's provisions we receive full and complete healing and abundant life. That's why for a practical illustration this historical account, which is not just a story, but are actual events that really happened, is so loaded, vital and powerful.

If we look on our problems and if we try to fix the problems it's not going to work on a permanent basis. We'll be preoccupied with our problems instead of objective truth. Objective truth will always guide our eyes to the solution of our problems, which is Jesus Christ. He will take care of it, because He promised that He would. There is no question about it, that a clear focus on Jesus Christ is definitely the only answer to deal with our problems effectively. A supernatural solution is always better and more powerful than a natural one. It's not an escape route, but rather a proper, healthy and truly effective way to deal with those problems. To focus on the problems can only kill us. To focus on Jesus Christ will energize us to be above things and to have things taken care of supernaturally with the best solution possible.

That's how life-changing things happen and how problems get really solved permanently. That's how we rid ourselves from nasty habits. It's not that we do anything, besides making positive choices to take our eyes off of our problems and to look directly unto Jesus for help. If we concentrate on Jesus, He'll be lifted up and magnified and our problems will become insignificant, as He takes care of them and guides us to deal with these things effectively according to His wisdom. It's really that simple and it works. Many people never experience this phenomenal truth and supernatural action. They are preoccupied with solving their natural problems, which often become energized by supernatural powers, in their own natural strength. They just can't keep their eyes focused on Jesus Christ, but instead always want to look back down on their problems that may have already gone away.

It's similar to the principle we've discussed earlier in this book about trying to change the unchangeable. Once you take your eyes off the problem it's history, relax and let God take care of it, and continue to focus with full concentration on Jesus Christ, which you'll do when you hear and study the Word of God. Victory is only a choice away. No matter how much or how little faith you've got, just look unto Jesus and that's it. If we hear and study the Word of God on a continuous basis, it will become much easier to trust God for all the details of our life, because we'll see God in action day after day.

1   2 Corinthians 10:5, The Amplified Bible

2   Philippians 4:8, NASB

3   Psalm 101:3, KJV

4   Isaiah 45:22, KJV

5   Numbers 21:6, The Amplified Bible

6   Numbers 21:9, The Amplified Bible

ABUNDANT LIFE

God wants every child of God to have an abundant life. "I came that they may have and enjoy life, and have it in abundance (to the full, till it overflows)."₁ You can see that it is very obvious that pure Christianity has nothing to do with religious structures of lifeless formalities. It's not a head trip either. Pure Christianity is fun because it works without ourselves trying to accomplish something. In fact we only watch God in action and we're the beneficiaries of His impartation and bestowment of blessings. The above verse says that Jesus Christ came so that we may have life and enjoy it.

"He who believes in Me [who cleaves to and trusts in and relies on Me] as the Scripture has said, From his innermost being shall flow [continuously] springs and rivers of living water."₂ This condition does not suggest that depression has any part in the life of such an individual. God can effectively heal depression and provide protection against the onslaught of depression. In fact, God will provide to every individual who is simply willing to accept God's life, pure happiness with utmost joy. Once again, there is nothing an individual can do within the realm of their own strength to receive the life of God, but we must simply be available to receive His life, which is done by making a choice to hear the Word of God. "This is my comfort in my affliction, That Thy word has revived me."₃

God doesn't want religious fanatics that roam the streets. But he wants people that are filled with His

Spirit and to whom He can give life more abundantly. This life is not acquired by "good" behavior or by some strange religious practice or exercise, but simply by being available to receive it. By a positive choice to hear the Word of God this life is imparted to us and we will say, "As for God, His way is perfect! The word of the Lord is tested and tried; He is a shield to all those who take refuge and put their trust in Him."4 In other words, "It really works."

To make it even easier for us to experience this abundant life and to keep in the flow of godly things, and to be continuously filled with the Holy Spirit, God will give us a brand new heart. "And I will take the stony [unnaturally hardened] heart out of their flesh, and will give them a heart of flesh [sensitive and responsive to the touch of their God]." Only God can do this change of heart, and He did it at the moment we trusted in Jesus Christ as our Savior for the eternal salvation of our soul. It's one act followed by so many beautiful things. God does it all. We just watch Him do it and we receive it and enjoy the benefits thereof.

1   John 10:10, The Amplified Bible
2   John 7:38, The Amplified Bible
3   Psalm 119:50, NASB
4   Psalm 18:30, The Amplified Bible
5   Ezekiel 11:19, The Amplified Bible

7

ABSOLUTE DELIVERANCE, FREEDOM AND VICTORY

We're all looking for some type of deliverance in our life of something that is really bugging us. Maybe it's a certain habit that we just can't shake off, or maybe it's a relationship in the workplace or in the family or neighborhood that really puts a lot of strain on us. Or maybe it's the finances that may preoccupy us, because week after week we work hard and seemingly we can't get out of debt and the bills are barely paid, living from one paycheck to the next one. Or maybe we just have too much money and we've finally bought all the toys that we were longing for, but permanent happiness didn't come with the toys.

We all have the inherent desire to be free. But free from what? There are a lot of pressures to keep up with the status symbols of society. We think that by changing certain things we'll be free. True, it probably can't hurt to change a few things in our lives. But if we go to the bottom of this freedom desire we find out that we just want to be free from the limitations of our physical body and all that comes with it.

We also have the need to experience victory in our lives. That's why we enter into competitions to provide the opportunity to become a winner and to experience victory.

In this chapter we'll go through some available options and practical applications of how to experience absolute deliverance, freedom and victory not dependent on our own performance nor the reactions or responses of others.

DELIVERANCE

As you know by now this book opens with a promise on deliverance, "He sent His word, . . . and delivered them from their destructions."[1] The Word of God is full of promises of deliverance. "He will deliver his soul from going into the pit, and his life shall see the light."[2] "For thou hast delivered my soul from death: wilt not thou deliver my feet from falling."[3]

Some people always try program A and B and C, etc., but while some programs may work to some extent temporarily, these programs usually never provide deliverance from something on a permanent basis. To obtain any results in and from these programs it normally takes very hard work, because these programs are natural provisions. Some suggestions in these programs might be interesting and helpful, but why give something with only a factor of chance a try, when on the other hand full deliverance is available free of charge without any effort on our part?

People also say, "Well, you've got to be realistic." Okay, what's realistic about trying a number of various self-help programs, wasting a lot of money and energy, resulting in virtually no visible positive results, even after many years, and putting you through a struggle? It doesn't make any sense to discuss this type of realism, because it's living in a superficial world of presumption and false expectations. Check out what God says in His Word about deliverance. The focus is what He can do for us, because He is the only One that can do anything effectively and with lasting results.

> "I waited patiently for the Lord; And
> He inclined to me, and heard my cry.
> He brought me up out of the pit of
> destruction, out of the miry clay; And
> He set my feet upon a rock making
> my footsteps firm. And He put a new
> song in my mouth, a song of praise
> to our God."[4]

Whatever the pit of destruction may be, He is able to bring us out of there. The rock is Jesus Christ and that's why our footsteps will be firm, because He is the unshakable rock. It also speaks of permanency—results that will last forever.

"I sought the Lord, and he heard me, and delivered me from all my fears. This poor man cried, and the Lord heard him, and saved him out of all his troubles."[5] This solution sounds pretty clear and definite to me. It can't get any better than this. This principle applies to every area of our life.

What about finances? We find several interesting accounts in the Bible where God delivered people from the devastating effects of an overload of debt, or just simply the deliverance from poverty or a personal famine. These historical accounts explain God's unfailing character towards us. If we turn to Him He will always have a solution ready for us.

In 1 Kings 17:8-16 we read about a widow woman

that had a very bleak outlook on the rest of her life. Elijah, a man of God, went to a certain village and was instructed by God to meet a certain widow woman there. When he found her, he first checked out if she was responsive to the Word of God by asking her for a little drinking water. Then he requested a small loaf of bread from her, but she responded by saying that she had only a handful of flour in a bowl and a little oil in a bottle. She also said that she was just going about to bake this little bit so that she and her son could eat it and die. Seemingly all hope was gone and the focus of this widow was only on the natural circumstances.

Anyway, Elijah first brought relaxation to the situation by saying that she shouldn't fear. Then he said that he still would like a little cake and she should prepare it for him first, and afterwards for herself and her son. He also spoke the Word of God which promised that there will be sufficient flour and oil for her household for many days. The account tells us that the flour wasted not and the bottle of oil was never empty.

As we have also read before, the Word of God will bring comfort to our soul and relax the atmosphere. Then God will take care of the situation and may very well involve you in the solution so that you can experience on site, so to speak, the blessings that come from His actions and are prepared for you.

While it's our obligation to handle finances in a responsible manner, especially when it concerns other peoples' money, we may have made some mistakes and are just seemingly unable to get out of the vicious cycle of debt. It's like a heavy weight put on us and the weekly or monthly payments are just impossible to meet. God has a solution for this problem, too.

We have a tremendous account about God's debt redemption plan in 2 Kings 4:1-7. Once again there is a widow and she cried out to God, and in this case specifically to the man of God called Elisha. She told him that the creditor had come to take her two sons to be his slaves. Back then they took the children when someone couldn't pay their debt. Elisha asked her what she had left, and she replied by saying that she had only a pot of oil left. He instructed her to borrow as many vessels from her neighbors as were available. She did so and brought all the vessels into the house and all vessels were filled supernaturally with oil. When all the vessels were full of oil she went to the man of God, Elisha, and told him about it. Elisha told her to sell the oil and to pay off her debt, and she and her sons should live from the rest.

That's certainly a nice retirement plan. By considering the natural circumstances she would have been unable to pay off her debt and would have lost her children. But by turning to God, trusting in Him and His supernatural provisions, God was able to go to work and to take care of the problem. Does this sound irrational? Does this sound just too good to be true? Well, I've seen this principle literally happen in front of my eyes, when a man had a tremendous debt and he was faithful in making his payments month after month for several years. His priorities were back in order, but those monthly payments and the remaining debt were a tremendous burden to him. He cried out to the Lord asking Him for help and when he went to the bank to check how much the remaining balance of the debt was, he was shocked to find out that only about two hundred dollars were needed to pay off the debt completely. In his estimate there was still a huge amount that had to be paid off, but after the bank checked all records for weeks and everything was carefully examined, the result was still the same—he only owed this two hundred bucks, that was it. Nobody knew about his debt and nobody paid it off and it didn't disappear by mistake, but it was God who took care of it supernaturally. Besides this certain testimony we've witnessed and heard of many examples that when people turn to God, He is able to do literal miracles—things that normally do not happen and are happening because of supernatural intervention.

1 Psalm 107:20, KJV
2 Job 33:28, KJV
3 Psalm 56:13, KJV
4 Psalm 40:1-3, NASB
5 Psalm 34:4, 6, KJV

FREEDOM

"So if the Son liberates you [makes you free men], then you are really and unquestionably free."₁ We all long for freedom. We may buy fast cars, or motorcycles, or go on a roller coaster or a skydiving experience just to get a glimpse of what freedom must feel like.

"For the law of the Spirit of life in Christ Jesus hath made me free from the law of sin and death."₂ "Where the Spirit of the Lord is, there is liberty."₃ "Stand fast therefore in the liberty wherewith Christ hath made us free."₄ Never do we want to go back to the bondage from which Jesus Christ has delivered us and has set us free. We're no longer under the performance pressures of society. Yes, at work we give our best and do the best possible job, and by the grace of God we'll be able to do it. We no longer have to give in to the pressures of sin and bad habits, because the grace of God "trained us to reject and renounce all ungodliness (irreligion) and worldly (passionate) desires."₅

The Word of God will make us free. Sin will always put us back into bondage, that's why "Thy word I have treasured in my heart, That I may not sin against Thee."₆ True freedom leads us to a victorious life. Free from the bondage and the devastating effects and consequences of sin; free from the rules and restrictions of weird concepts and philosophies that were trying to oppress us by forcing their unbalanced standards on us. No longer do we need to be intimidated or manipulated by subjective individuals and by people that have ulterior motives. Together with the Word of God, the Holy Spirit will provide us with discernment in specific situations. Without much hassle we will know what the right thing to do will be in a situation. Our mind will become pretty sharp and perceptive and aware of things that harass us trying to get us back into bondage and that try to take away our divine freedom.

Even the self-righteous crowd that is seemingly so "perfect" and has seemingly everything in order, are often so proud and arrogant as they parade their achievements. In doing so they continuously knock people down and destroy the self-esteem of others, which is the only way they'll be able to feel better than someone else.

What a contrast when Jesus said, "The Spirit of the Lord is upon me, because he hath anointed me to preach the gospel to the poor; he hath sent me to heal the brokenhearted, to preach deliverance to the captives, and recovering of sight to the blind, to set at liberty them that are bruised."[7]

True freedom brings relief and rest to our soul. Jesus preached deliverance, freedom and victory. He spoke encouraging words when he said, "Come unto me all ye that labor and are heavy laden, and I will give you rest. Take my yoke upon you, and learn of me; for I am meek and lowly in heart: and ye shall find rest unto your souls. For my yoke is easy, and my burden is light."[8]

1   John 8:36, The Amplified Bible

2   Romans 8:2, KJV

3   2 Corinthians 3:17, KJV

4   Galatians 5:1, KJV

5   Titus 2:12, The Amplified Bible

6   Psalm 119:11, NASB

7   Luke 4:18, KJV

8   Matthew 11:28-30, KJV

VICTORY

We all long for a victorious and successful life. But what is true success and how can we obtain genuine victory? People have all kinds of definitions to describe victory. The Word of God defines victory for a person in many passages. One of the essential passages for victory deals with what God will equip a person with to walk through life victoriously. These things are called the fruit of the Holy Spirit. "But the fruit of the [Holy] Spirit [the work which His presence within accomplishes] is love, joy (gladness), peace, patience (an even temper, forbearance), kindness, goodness (benevolence), faithfulness, Gentleness (meekness, humility), self-control (self-restraint, continence)."[1] Equipped with the fruit of the Holy Spirit life will become very victorious in the ultimate sense of the word.

"But they that wait upon the Lord shall renew their strength; they shall mount up with wings as eagles; they shall run, and not be weary; and they shall walk, and not faint."[2] Based on the fruit of the Holy Spirit which is a gift from God, it's therefore also God who enables us to wait upon Him. Waiting upon Him has lots of benefits as just described in the above verse. The eagle soars without exerting any energy at all, and it is the only bird that can look directly at the sun and not injure its eyes.

As we grow in the grace and knowledge of our Lord and Savior, Jesus Christ, our life will be a celebration and manifestation of inherent victory. Even though we may fail in one area or the other at times, this type of failure doesn't take away from our victorious life. It's only when we dwell on failures—often these are only very small and actually insignificant mistakes, but of course, also includes the big mistakes—that the spirit of defeat is given entrance and territory to do its destructive work.

Depression has no part in a truly victorious life. There might be attacks at times and thought projections, but the Word of God in me empowered by the Holy Spirit is able to destroy such vain imaginations immediately and claim instant victory. If we don't have the Word of God stored in the rooms of our soul, then when the attacks come the Holy Spirit is unable to recall and use the Word as a sword which would provide us with accurate discernment. If the Word of God is not residing in our soul, our memory system would recall a mental frame of reference and various reactions that do not originate with God, but are earthly, dragging us down. It's when we allow ourselves to be carried away with negative thought projections by feeding upon them that a spirit of depression is able to come in and destroy us strategically step by step.

Satan uses depression as a very powerful tool with all kinds of people. A person that doesn't believe in God is virtually unable to obtain true victory, because to what or whom would such a person look for receiving victory? There wouldn't be any promise or actual hope for genuine victory, if victory would depend on a person's own performance, accomplishments and strength. A natural victory is only temporary, while divine supernatural victory is permanent because the victory doesn't depend on the individual, but on what God Almighty has already accomplished for us which, of course, always has eternal results. The moment we believe in Jesus Christ as our Savior we become partakers of His victory and are enabled to enjoy the results of this divine victory completely.

"For whatever is born of God is victorious over the world; and this is the victory that conquers the world, even our faith. Who is it that is victorious over [that conquers] the world but he who believes that Jesus is the Son of God [who adheres to, trusts in, and relies on that fact]?"3 As we hear the Word of God, genuine faith is imparted to us, meaning we become partakers of God's mind and therefore the Holy Spirit is able to function properly in us. The temporal value system with all its earthly concepts, social pressures and ideas won't be able to involve us anymore with these things that would consistently try to defeat us—unless we choose to and want to within the realm of our free volition.

That's when absolute deliverance and freedom turns

into true and permanent victory. "But thanks be to God, Who gives us the victory [making us conquerors] through our Lord Jesus Christ."[4] Not even death can scare a true Christian, because as recipients of Eternal Life at the very moment of salvation, each and every born-again Christian will never die, but instead will live forever. The Scriptures reflecting on this truth ask, "O death, where is thy sting? O grave, where is thy victory?"[5] For the Christian death no longer is something he has to fear, because he has overcome death through Jesus Christ and therefore also resurrection is a guaranteed and sure fact.

This type of victory is final with permanent results. If we accept this eternal fact, we'll be able to experience this victory in our emotions already here on earth. Based on eternal truth we're absolutely invincible. While outward circumstances may seemingly at times indicate otherwise, inside we can rest assured that the battle has been won by the Lord Jesus Christ Himself, and that the victory is ours no matter what.

1   Galatians 5:22-23, The Amplified Bible
2   Isaiah 40:31, KJV
3   1 John 5:4-5, The Amplified Bible
4   1 Corinthians 15:57, The Amplified Bible
5   1 Corinthians 15:55, KJV

8

THE SUPERNATURAL REALITY

E very breath we take is a supernatural experience. Individuals are energized by supernatural forces. Everything we think and do is either energized by the Kingdom of God or by the kingdom of Satan. Both of these supernatural forces are constantly at war. As humans we are caught in the middle of it and no wonder we're interested in the supernatural world that encompasses us. Satan is already defeated and has lost the war, but still he doesn't believe it and will try to convince us otherwise until his judgement is finally executed at the end of time.

While we like to dabble in our thought life through strange books and movies into the supernatural, we often don't want to think of the supernatural phenomena as a reality, because somehow we just don't believe that this supernatural world really exists. We think the supernatural world is mysterious and cannot be explained. But the basics are very simple and can be explained quite easily. In this chapter we want to explore and touch on a few topics a lot of people are interested in. These are themes that are usually never defined precisely and are explained only vaguely with abstract concepts leaving plenty of room for our imaginations to go wild and to consider all kinds of possibilities without firm convictions.

The supernatural world, while most of the time invisible, is just as real as the natural world. And it's the dark supernatural forces that intensify and even cause depression trying to destroy us. On the other hand, God provides supernatural deliverance and victory from these supernatural bondages, slavery and effects.

HELL

In our modern world the real literal hell described in the Bible seems to be a very abstract place and virtually nonexistent. People call certain environments and life situations on earth hell, but while certain environments and life situations can be very nasty and painful they surely don't even come close and do not even provide a glimpse into what the real hell revealed in objective truth really is. Hell is a very real place. One basic description or definition would be to say that hell is a place far removed from the presence of God without the possibility of ever changing its eternal condition.

By studying the subject of hell in the Word of God we're able to receive at least a tiny vision of what hell must really be like. And just a tiny glimpse of a divine vision regarding hell will change our life forever, because we sure don't want to go there. Hell is not a party place. The Scriptures tell us that hell was prepared for Satan and his angels, and every human being that is cast into hell is an intruder in hell. It's not going to be fun to be in hell for all eternity. The Bible tells us that it's a terrible place where there is continuous darkness and absolute loneliness, but where continuous screaming and unimaginable pain exist. It feels like the body is eaten up by Piranhas on a continuous basis without the possibility of any relief at any time. It feels like being continuously roasted without ever being taken off the barbecue. The conscience never ceases and throughout all eternity each individual in hell will be reminded about all the opportunities they had to simply accept Jesus Christ as their personal Savior, but they rejected Him each time. It will go on for all eternity without the possibility of ever changing this horrible destiny.

Hell is described as a place where the passions of men are continuously present, but without the possibility of ever satisfying any of these lusts, not even in some measure. Imagine a continuous craving for something without ever being able to obtain any type of relief or satisfaction ever. It's a bottomless pit and it's like being in a constant state of a free fall being dragged down by very strong demonic forces and dark creatures never ever reaching solid ground and being unable to lose consciousness. It's a painful place and a terrible state to be in. Hell is a place far away from the presence of God and once an individual is cast into hell, this horrible destiny, it can never be changed—it's his or her eternal abode forever.

I once made a painting called "A Great Gulf Fixed" in which I've tried to illustrate just basically the difference between Heaven and hell. In hell there are flames and only screaming faces expressing unimaginable pain. On the other hand, in Heaven individuals are shown with a glorified body as they will shine throughout eternity in the presence of God Almighty. Obviously, no painting or description can ever express or translate the fathomless sorrow and pain of hell nor the incomprehensible Glory of Heaven.

Is God still a loving God by sending a person to hell? Yes, He is always amazingly gracious and loving at all times. God in His infinite mercy and grace made a provision for mankind so that every person in the world can spend eternity in His presence. In fact, He doesn't want anybody to perish, but would like everyone to be saved. He has sent His Son, Jesus Christ, and He has sent His Word and the Holy Spirit to teach us and understand truth. He also gave each person a measure of faith and a God-consciousness. God doesn't want robots or machines and that's why He equipped every

person with a free will. While God may lovingly motivate us so that we will make a positive decision for Him
and also in creation has made His handiwork visible
and accessible to us, He cannot force Himself on anyone.
Each person must make a choice to let God deliver them
from the power of darkness and translate them into the
kingdom of His dear Son, which happens at the moment
of salvation. People just need to believe in Jesus Christ
as their personal Savior and their eternal destiny will
be Heaven and not hell.

It's a reality that not everybody will spend eternity
in the presence of God, but that multitudes will go to
hell by their own choice—teenagers included. Yes, it's
their own choice to go to hell, not as a penalty for their
sins, but because of rejecting throughout their life in
their free volition the only way of salvation, Jesus
Christ. Sin was paid for by Jesus Christ on the cross of
Calvary and therefore sin is no longer an issue. Many
people make a lot of wrong choices throughout their
lives. While salvation is available to everybody, no
matter what their current lifestyle may be, and they
don't even have to change to receive Jesus Christ as
their personal Savior, it is often their lifestyle within
the realm of all kinds of habitual sins that will keep
them from accepting Jesus Christ. Often there is guilt
and the deception that an individual isn't good enough
for God, or in the other case that the person doesn't need
God, which in both cases is a lie. Every person can come
to God just the way they are and everybody needs a
personal relationship with the Creator. It could also be,

humanly speaking, a good religious lifestyle following a false philosophy and never ever trusting in Jesus Christ as the sole Savior and therefore ending up in hell. Jesus Christ is the only door into Heaven—there is none other.

Consider this, it's not worth it to waste the few years that we have here on earth when eternity is such a long time and will never ever end. What are seventy years or so compared to billions and billions of years? This short time on earth is such a very important time for each and every individual. It's an opportunity to get to know God and to receive the free gift of salvation to secure our eternal destiny in His presence.

It doesn't make sense to be deceived by worldly philosophies that are full of speculations and abstract ideas. These philosophies may appease the conscience to some degree temporarily, but in the end they leave every single follower stranded with the reality of an eternal destiny in hell as a result. Hell is a very real place and is only something to be scared of when you don't have Jesus Christ as your personal Savior.

Time is very short and we could run out of time any day now. It's time we stop fooling around and settle some very important and essential issues in our life as long as we still have time to do so. Nobody knows, but God alone, when it's time to go and when time will have run out for each one of us. Once it's over our eternal destiny can no longer be changed—it's final. If you haven't accepted Jesus Christ as your personal Savior yet, don't you think it's time to do so right now, just in case?

SATAN

Is the devil just a myth or is he really a being that "Roams around like a lion roaring [in fierce hunger], seeking someone to seize upon and devour?"₁ If the devil is real, what does he look like and what's his agenda and purpose? A long time ago, the devil or Satan was a beautiful angel full of wisdom in Heaven in the presence of God. Back then his name was Lucifer and he was a perfect creation. As such Lucifer received a free volition, but he was just a creation, made perfect by God Himself. To clarify some speculations, humans do not become angels and angels while they may take on the form of a human being at times, they certainly cannot become humans in their intrinsic nature. True, humans may appear to be angels and angels may appear in human form, nevertheless their nature or creation of being either an angel or a human being doesn't change.

Objective truth has quite a bit to say about Lucifer and his tactics, etc. He was perfect in every sense of the word. God created beings such as angels and humans and equipped them with a free will, so that they have the freedom of choice and the ability to make decisions as free volitional beings. Each choice has consequences. Positive decisions towards God produce phenomenal results, effects and consequences by receiving tremendous blessings from God. Decisions against God will also produce results, effects and consequences by the lack of availability of blessings from God. God doesn't owe anything to anybody, so the bestowment of blessings on an individual is an act of grace.

Making negative decisions against God's perfect will causes the disruption of fellowship with God. We must remember God is the Creator and we are the creatures. No table ever became self-willed and said to the carpenter who made him, "Carpenter I don't need you anymore and I have decided to establish my own carpentry shop." We're of course more than just a table, but in principle we've been created and we are not self-existent like God. I know it may be very hard to comprehend, but God has never been created—He is the Creator. He has always been in existence and created everything. He made us in His image and He gave to us humans a free will and He also gave to the angels free volition. Compared to humans, the angels were created in a perfect state and therefore the death of Christ on the cross of Calvary is not available for the forgiveness of sins committed by angels. Only human beings benefit from Christ's death on that certain cross.

Lucifer was perfectly beautiful and full of wisdom—and one day he looked at himself and his tasks and achievements as the chief angel, and he thought that he could be like God. But Lucifer was just a creature and he was not the Creator. Lucifer said that he would exalt his throne above the stars of God and he would be like the most High (God). At this point he made a negative decision against God and suffered the consequences of such a bad choice that certain blessings were no longer available to him.

Lucifer took his case, of God being seemingly unfair

to him, to the other angels and one third of the angels also made a negative decision against God and accepted Lucifer as their leader and god. The fellowship with God was broken and since Lucifer crusaded in rebellion against God, judgment was passed down on him. God cannot look upon sin and therefore He must judge sin and remove sin from His presence. That's what happened and Lucifer was cast out of Heaven.

Today, Satan is the prince of the power of the air and together with the fallen angels he has established a counterfeit kingdom. He deceives people and spreads lies trying to keep human beings away from accepting Jesus Christ as their Savior. Satan knows that once a person is saved that this person no longer belongs to him. Sure, he will attack the Christian after their salvation also, because a true born-again Christian is dangerous to his kingdom by spreading the news, the Gospel of Jesus Christ, so that even more people can be saved.

Satan knows that he has lost, but doesn't want to believe it. He knows that his time is short and finally his ultimate judgment of being cast into the lake of fire— hell—is near. His goal is to get people preoccupied with anything that keeps them away from focusing on Jesus Christ. He attacks us with thought projections manipulating our emotions and energizing us with a self-centered lifestyle, whatever this may mean in each individual case. Of Satan is said that "The thief comes only to steal, and kill, and destroy."[2]

Compared to unsaved people, Christians have the

advantage of being indwelt by the Holy Spirit and therefore demon possession is not possible in the case of a Christian. But for the born-again Christian who doesn't study the Word of God properly, it is possible that he can be demonically oppressed. Unsaved people are in constant danger of being possessed by demons— potentially even by a multitude of demons.

Satan's appearance may not always be the obvious bad looking beast or guy who is into drugs, or whatever, but he frequently appears also as an angel of light. Of course, he is not the angel of light, but he disguises himself as such and it could be human righteousness and goodness that he may use to distract people to keep them away from Jesus Christ. In Catholicism we frequently see cultic Mary worship and that's, of course, an invention from the devil. While Mary was the earthly mother of Jesus and was probably a very good person humanly speaking, she certainly cannot redeem anyone, because the way, the truth and the life is Jesus Christ alone. Jesus Christ died for the sins of the whole world and not Mary. Jesus Christ was the only acceptable sacrifice for our sins. Mary called Jesus Christ "Lord."

Satan's sin was independence of God and exaltation of self and his thoughts are self-centered. It's very obvious in our world today that he's been quite successful in spreading his philosophy throughout the world. Often it will appear that what Satan does is so good, humanly speaking, but in the end leaves people desperately in the lurch. Buddhism too, is a self-centered religion. Also the Jewish faith keeps people away from Jesus Christ and so does the Muslim religion. Even in Christianity there are those that teach a self-centered religion which is just another philosophy that has nothing to do with pure Christianity, even though they may use parts of the Bible and the name of Jesus Christ. You could go through all philosophies in existence and all you need to look for is if this or that is self-centered and if it is a self-help program of man trying to please God, or if the teachings are Christ-centered and a free gift situation of what God has done for mankind already.

Every thought is either from Satan's kingdom or from the Kingdom of God. Satan cannot read our mind, but he can read the reactions of our emotions in facial expressions, etc. He can project thoughts and stimulate certain thought patterns that are apart from objective truth. Satan may even use bits and pieces of objective truth, but will always fall short of presenting the whole truth and therefore will always try to deceive us.

How is it possible for us to be protected from the devastating effects of the devil's attacks? It's once again objective truth that will be our protection. Even Jesus Christ was attacked by Satan and Jesus used the Word of God to destroy his attacks. When we agree with the Word of God and apply it, the devil will flee from us. Satan will come back again and again trying to deceive us and trying to wear us out, but when we resist him with the Word of God he will always flee from us and he will not be able to succeed. The more we grow into spiritual maturity the more angry Satan will become at us and his attacks will become more subtle and canny than ever before. But he's a loser and because he is defeated already, ultimately he can't win.

It's a fact that Satan is very real and active in our world today and in everyday life. At age eight I got really scared for the first time when I watched the original "Dr. Frankenstein" movie and I thought it was an innocent film about doctors and a hospital. The next thing I really got scared of, was a television report on heart attacks and at around the age of eight or nine I couldn't go to sleep, because I thought I would die that night of a heart attack. I was really frightened with an experience I had around the age of twelve or so, when I first dabbled with rock music and some science fiction literature. In the middle of the night I went from my room into the small hallway of our apartment trying to go to the bathroom. Suddenly, as I opened the door in front of me were demonic creatures similar to the "Iron Maiden" record covers many years ago. I closed my eyes several times and when I opened them these creatures didn't go away. They stood there what seemed to be a long desert corridor trying to grab me, but they couldn't touch me. I finally let go of a scream and walked away and the distinctive image disappeared. I was really scared from then on and I believed that there was a supernatural world even though I had no definition of what such world consisted of. Almost every day we had to go down into the basement of our apartment building and it was always a very unpleasant experience to say the least.

With all the images that our kids are presented with on television, in video games, etc. on a daily basis, it's not only understandable that many children have nightmares, but also it should be very obvious that Satan is actively at work already in the little ones. He's trying to project thoughts that are from his kingdom to destroy individuals, starting even in small children.

It's crucial to kneel down with your child at bedtime and say a simple prayer requesting protection for a calm and healthy sleep. In cases of bad nightmares, it was reported that Christian praise music played softly during the night prevented nightmares in many cases. Of course, if nightmares are a problem, you must do away with all television programs, literature, toys and music, etc. that deal with or contain such scary characters and story lines. We must take these things seriously, because we're obligated to protect our young children from the influence of demons and Satan himself.

Some people will take it to an extreme now and will go on a witch-hunt and certainly that's not appropriate either. Sure, we need absolute convictions, but we also need a proper balance, otherwise we're rapidly back in bondage and are locked up into a cage. One interesting thing the living Word of God will do is to lead us and guide us specifically through the Holy Spirit in what is an appropriate measure and what isn't. This takes the guesswork out of a lot of things leaving us free to live an abundant life. It's so good to study the Word of God in categories, because it will make us free and deliver us from false concepts and strange mind games, etc.

1   1 Peter 5:8, The Amplified Bible

2   John 10:10, NASB

PSYCHICS • UFOs AND ALIENS

Throughout most of my teenage years I believed somewhat in the existence of UFOs. For years I planned on
building my own spaceship to explore the universe some
day in the future. Then in the eighties during my
various extensive studies I also came across the UFO
phenomenon. The result was amazing: UFOs may very
well exist. But the explanation of why aliens and UFOs
exist was much more intriguing. As Satan frequently
disguises himself and his army of demons is consistently plotting one attack of distraction after the other
on mankind, the UFO-and-Alien scheme is just another
way of distracting people from the real issues in life. Of
course, these UFOs are not really beings from another
planet, but are fallen angels which are demons playing
their games on earth as long as they're permitted to do
so.

Even the appearance of an alien life-form is certainly nothing else than simply the unique appearance
of demons. Demons are fallen angels. They are disem-
bodied spirits and they're able to inhabit all kinds of
various bodies to appear to mankind. They can also

project distinctive images trying to manipulate the mind. Aliens and UFOs should be the least of our worries. Objective truth doesn't say anything about other beings on other planets, but instead talks about the human race and the animals here on earth and also about the various types of heavenly angels, including the fallen angels and their demonic appearances in our world.

When it comes to psychics, the deceptive game continues. While only God has absolute foreknowledge of what is going to happen to each one of us and to the world in time, demons have only historical data, accumulated knowledge and experience available to them to potentially "predict" the future based on historical facts. To "predict" future events is simply nothing more than the ability to somehow properly read and understand historical data regarding the accumulation of knowledge and experience within the realm of a highly potential possibility in the future.

For many years I've done various tests on this subject and was able to predict the direction of the stock market pretty accurately—even regarding the movement of certain individual stocks. These predictions weren't perfect and sometimes the timing was off by a few months, or in some stocks certain things happened that were unpredictable and sent the stock price in the opposite direction producing a terrible stock-price performance. But considering everything, any casual observer back then may have thought that in most cases we have had a crystal ball. At that time we were able to predict the direction of the stock market, including some specific stocks very accurately. In October of 1990, we talked about a 50% increase in the Dow Jones from the 2400 level to approx. 3500 within a couple of years. In 1991, we discussed the strong possibility of a Dow heading potentially towards 5000 within just a few years. In 1997, the Dow Jones crossed the 8000 mark before correcting in the fourth quarter of that year.

Now everybody will ask what we think may happen in the U.S. stock market in the years to come. Potentially the stock market will continue to go up with a few breathers and corrections in between—maybe even with a year in neutral. Unless something dramatic happens, which is potentially always a possibility because of the late stage in history we're in, and because of biblical prophecy regarding the final years of human history, it is very much possible that the Dow has the potential to climb to 15,000 and beyond until the early part of the new millennium. Considering the global marketplace and new markets such as China alone with a population of 1.2 billion people, U.S. companies have a tremendous economical advantage and edge to penetrate such megamarkets and to propel U.S. stock markets into stratospheric heights, which no one can imagine today. All of this, however, is not looking with a clear view into the future, seeing a vision of future events literally unfolding in front of our eyes as many people want you to believe. It's all just based on reading and understanding historical data regarding the accumulation of knowledge and experience within the realm of a highly potential possibility in the future.

A real psychic is a medium used by demons. Since demons have been around for thousands and thousands of years their knowledge and experience is extensive—they've seen it all, so to speak. We have to understand that there are a lot of so called psychics that just want to make some money and play a psychological game and are, in fact, simply frauds and rip-offs.

There is also the other kind of psychics. They have actually given themselves over to the powers of darkness and are used by demons to once again manipulate through thought projections the minds of individuals. People are in awe if someone else they've never met can tell them things about their life and their unique life experiences. Well, consider that there are millions of demons and they watch a lot of people continuously and literally keep an updated database of each human being on file. It's easy for them to know the life experiences of an individual and then use a psychic to speak to these individuals. The moment a common trust is established the client is very vulnerable and open to any kind of mind manipulation. The psychic may use the traditional method of "predicting" a potential possibility in the future because of what is known about the client from the knowledge of the database the demon communicated. Often a demon will project thoughts and suggest certain future events so that these future events may even become reality. The goal of the demon, of course, is to destroy this certain individual and to distract him or her from trusting in Jesus Christ, so that instead they put their faith into the psychic and his or her "predictions."

When therefore future events are "predicted" through a psychic, and as our minds focus on these "predictions" to see them come true, these future events may possibly actually happen. The reason being, our concentration and energy is bundled towards that certain direction and it is our ego that will make these things in some way come to pass. In a sense the psychic is a type of motivator. All these "predictions," of course, are not real predictions at all.

God doesn't want us to consult psychics, but instead He wants us to consult His Word which enables Him to act with the full force and power of His Kingdom on our behalf as we trust in Him. Once again, instead of limited self-effort and dangerous demonic activity, we can come relaxed to Jesus Christ and watch Him answer our prayers. We can trust in Him and He will take care of our problems. As we learned earlier in this book, true faith can move mountains and there is no need to know the future nor to seek the advice of a demonic medium to fulfill our purpose in life and to enjoy a fulfilled life. The counsel of psychics will only harm us and confirm the stronghold that Satan has on our life if we rely on such weird and ungodly counsel.

In the Bible we read the historical account of King Saul who despite the precise will of God consulted a psychic and was foretold in this psychic session that he and his three sons would die shortly thereafter. The historical records tell us that the three sons of King Saul died and that King Saul committed suicide shortly after the visit to the psychic. The psychic was called a witch and destruction and death followed the psychic session. Not a bad example and lesson to learn from.

As we study the Word of God and let the Holy Spirit make it alive to us, God may very well show us visions of who He is and what He can do, and possibly even of future events. All of these godly visions will be in absolute accordance with the full counsel of God revealed in the Scriptures. This is how we can actually determine if a vision is truly from God or not—every vision from God must be based on the principles taught and found in the Word of God. If something is not in accordance with the Word of God, then it is simply not of God and therefore it is better for us to discard such a thing immediately.

ANGELS

As we've just discussed in this chapter there are really angels in existence today. God created angels and they're very real beings. We have the fallen angels that followed Satan, who himself is an angel, and who rebelled against God and were cast out of Heaven. Then we have the good angels, so to speak, that were not deceived and exercised their free will to agree with God and stay with God.

God's angels have various functions and often they're

messengers or are sent to minister to us. The Word of God explains the purpose and tasks of angels in detail. I believe that each one of us has at least one guardian angel during our life here on earth. If you look at your life carefully you will remember certain situations in which you experienced the supernatural protection of a guardian angel. Maybe it was an accident or a potential accident and only through a miracle did you not get hurt or killed. Watch children play on the playground and you'll quickly believe in guardian angels.

LUCK

Just for the record, I personally do not believe in luck and I don't think there is such a thing called luck. But I do believe in blessings which are bestowed upon us by God. Nobody is lucky, because luck is nonexistent. What is the reality of what we call luck? It could be that God may have blessed us specifically. Or it may be that a guardian angel protected us from something devastating or ministered unto us to get us through something more easily and even victoriously. Satan and his demons may lure us away from trusting in God by manipulating the system to seemingly provide us with an unexpected benefit. Satan's plot, however, will eventually lead us to destruction.

Did you ever notice that when people begin gambling for the first time they more often than not win a little bit. They call it beginners' luck. But in reality it is Satan's bait, because when you win once, subconsciously you think you can win again and again and hit it big some day. We've had many interviews with compulsive gamblers and this was the reason quoted most often according to their recollection of initial events why they continued to gamble. They really thought they could win again because they won initially when they first began to gamble. Of course, every person has a different background, etc. and in some cases the winning streak may last for weeks and months—just long enough until you're hooked. Once you're hooked Satan will project thoughts about your first winnings and impress your mind with these thoughts, and he will suggest that you'll make it sooner or later—just keep on playing. But the big day never comes and in between you lose your house, family, job, etc. and you become frustrated, angry and depressed, and in the end you're left destroyed. You bought into a lie and an illusion and wasted years or even your life believing it and to hunt after it.

Yes, one out of millions of people will win the lottery and occasionally someone will win in casinos, but don't be fooled, gaming is a gigantic business. Las Vegas in the Nevada desert didn't grow by most people winning money there, but instead was built from the accumulated losses from the majority of people that gambled there. No casino can survive if they give away more than they take in. Gaming is based upon deception no matter what games you play. Just around 1980, I frequented casinos in Europe and the U.S. Never did I think that I could depend on luck to pay my bills. The only games I was interested in were games in which the skill of the player could determine the outcome of the game. It was very hard work and not at all that easy to walk away a winner. Even with the skill nearly perfected certain surrounding circumstances and components of the game needed to play together and fall properly into place in order for me to win. But don't think you can apply any useful skill in lottery games, Keno, slot machines, and even in most card games and table games skill is not an issue, because the outcome of these games are not determined by skill.

I finally concluded that there are many other ways that are much easier to make a more predictable living. When I became a born-again Christian, over the years I also learned that while every person has a free volition and can do whatever they want no matter if it is beneficial or devastating to them or whatever, God encourages people to solely trust in Him for supplying their needs, to bless them in abundance and to take care of them—but a casino or gaming institution is certainly not the place where God will choose to bless us.

The supernatural is certainly an interesting subject and it is quite extensive. Objective truth shows us a whole array of specific demons and demon activities. In Scripture, thirty-four specific categories of demons are identified. There are demons that deceive and cause rebellion; there are demons of oppression, depression, betrayal, anger, murder, lunacy and destruction; and there are even demons of supernatural wisdom that perform miracles. The fall of Satan and the future execution of his judgement with his eternal destiny is also explained in detail in the Word of God. The Bible also describes Heaven to us and the reality and various functions of angels. In this book we were only able to touch a little bit on this mysterious and powerful world that makes each one of us a very active participant in it—no matter if we acknowledge it or not. An interesting fact about truth is that it doesn't matter if we believe or not and it doesn't depend on our opinion, because truth doesn't change and it's always true.

9

ULTIMATE PROSPERITY

We all desire to prosper in one way or the other. Some are searching for eternal youth and perfect health, others reach for the stars to obtain tremendous wealth and fame, or perhaps significance in the community or in the corporate hierarchy, and again others wish for prosperous relationships, and some also desire spiritual prosperity. What do you desire in life? Is it some of the above or is it most or even all of these things we just mentioned? You'll be astonished when I show you in this chapter that we can have it all and it's within our reach and available for virtually everybody.

BLESSINGS AND PROSPERITY

Life is a blessing. Every breath we take is a gift from God. We don't deserve a thing. Yes, we may work hard and make intelligent decisions, but everything we have and obtain is a gift from God—it's all a special favor we don't deserve. God gives us the air we breathe and He keeps us functioning so that our hearts continue to bump blood through our bodies.

There are certain things that we consider normal blessings. We often become familiar with these phenomenal gifts and even take them for granted. Even though these blessings are necessary to live, these are surely not to be taken for granted and are a special gift to each one of us moment by moment. All of these blessings can be defined under the umbrella of logistical grace. By honoring the laws of establishment certain benefits will be derived automatically. Most people today live within this framework of logistical grace.

But there is another aspect of blessings and these blessings are very specific blessings provided by God on a personal and particular level. Specific prayers answered can be combined in this category. It depends solely on the mercy and grace of God to receive such particular extraordinary blessings. Only a very few people on earth are in a position to receive such blessings, even though each person can be in such a position in a snap by simply exercising their free volition positively towards God. This is way beyond logistical grace, but blessings of this so called greater-grace magnitude are truly significant. Can you imagine that your prayers can be answered specifically, and sometimes even immediately?

The Bible is full with promises of what God can do specifically, if a person agrees with objective truth and accepts God's solutions, suggestions, etc.—simply His wisdom for problems, decisions and as a point of reference. Referring to the person that is listening to the man of God when the Word of God is preached and taught, it is said, "Believe his prophets, so shall ye prosper."[1] About the Word of God it is said that "It shall not return unto me void, but it shall accomplish that which I please, and it shall prosper in the thing whereto I sent it."[2]

Seeking and wishing for blessings and prosperity isn't wrong, instead it is absolutely appropriate to do so. Many people feel condemned whenever they desire something special or when they've worked hard and saved money to purchase certain material goods which may be considered luxury items. There is absolutely nothing wrong with it. "The love of money is the root of all evil."[3] In the improper pursuit of accumulating more money and material possessions there is self-destruction and the destruction of the lives around us. That's when depression creeps in, because frequently we're unable to fulfill our material wishes within the desired period of time. Then we become frustrated and eventually depressed, because we're not getting what we want.

When we're occupied with the things of God, He is able to bestow particular blessings upon us, because our priorities are in the right place and the blessings are no longer a distraction. Jesus said "But seek ye first the kingdom of God, . . . and all these things shall be added unto you."₄ "For where your treasure is, there will your heart be also."₅ Then we'll appreciate prosperity and blessings, because they are a gift from God which we receive, but didn't deserve. No longer is it necessary to keep up with the Joneses, but we're liberated and are finally able to enjoy genuine freedom from the bondages society is consistently trying to put on us. We don't care anymore if we have the nicest cars in our neighborhood, instead we appreciate nice cars and congratulate our neighbor who has these cars. There is nothing wrong with us having the nicest cars in the neighborhood either, but it's no longer an issue that puts unnecessary pressure on us to obtain such vehicles, even though we may have them in our driveway or garage.

Being set free in all of these little areas will lift a huge boulder from our shoulders and we'll feel free as a bird. Most of all, depression will no longer find entry into our life, because there is nothing that can be used by the demons of depression to lure us again into dangerous territory. Even if we're attacked in our minds with some devilish suggestions of all kinds of things, we've got the guard up which is a protective and impenetrable wall of objective truth.

"Beloved, I wish above all things that thou mayest prosper and be in health, even as thy soul prospereth."₆ You'll be in good health and you'll prosper when your soul is prospering. Your soul is prospering when you study the Word of God and let the Holy Spirit do His work in you. As we get older our physical health can deteriorate, because we have a body that will eventually die. It's a fragile body and every day of good health is an absolute gift from God. Even when we do not have physical health we can be in excellent spiritual health. Still, because I believe in the power of the Word of God and in the Grace of God and in a God who said that nothing shall be impossible for Him, I will always believe that everybody—no matter what their physical condition might be—can be healed in a moment. I believe that blind people can be healed and receive their sight again, and that cancer can go away in a snap, just like that.

Yes, I believe in miracles, because while I first just believed in the miraculous power of God based on the Word of God, during my life as a Christian I've seen all kinds of miracles happen in front of my eyes. Certainly we shouldn't become miracle crazy, but we just trust in a loving and caring Almighty God who really loves each one of us. He can do things we can't imagine. When Jesus Christ is lifted up, God is able to work through His Word and through the Holy Spirit. He will bring healing and deliver us from our destructions.

The emphasis should never be a focus on blessings and prosperity, nor to direct our efforts, attention and concentration towards these precious things. The focus must remain on Jesus Christ, because only then can the blessings be received. The following poem by Albert B. Simpson has put things properly in perspective.

"Once it was the blessing, now it is the
Lord;
Once it was the feeling, now it is His
Word.
Once His gifts I wanted, now the Giver
own;
Once I sought for healing, now Himself
alone.
Once 'twas painful trying, now 'tis
perfect trust;
Once a half salvation, now the uttermost.
Once 'twas ceaseless holding, now He
holds me fast;
Once 'twas constant drifting, now my
anchor's cast.
Once 'twas busy planning, now 'tis
trustful prayer;
Once 'twas anxious caring, now He
has the care.
Once 'twas what I wanted, now what
Jesus says;
Once 'twas constant asking, now 'tis
ceaseless praise.
Once it was my working, His it hence
shall be;
Once I tried to use Him, now He uses
me.
Once the power I wanted, now the
Mighty One;
Once for self I labored, now for Him

alone.
Once I hoped in Jesus, now I know He's
mine;
Once my lamps were dying, now they
brightly shine.
Once for death I waited, now His
coming hail;
And my hopes are anchored safe
within the veil."₇

We may not understand how it works, and people
try so hard to make their dreams come true, but once
certain priorities are set into the right order many of the
desires automatically become reality. These blessings
are a gift. People look for prosperity in all the wrong
places and sometimes some people are seemingly successful with the accumulation of material possessions
and stardom, but usually it's not the genuine thing. It's
so easy to get caught up in the rat race. If it's a self-made
prosperity, once a certain status is reached, it takes a lot
of effort to keep this status and to continue to advance.
Nobody can truly trust in themselves for obtaining
prosperity—it's all a gift from God.

There are two attitudes that we can take on. The
first one would be to look back and say that we did it all
and congratulate ourselves for our achievements. The
second attitude would be to thank God for everything
He did and provided. At times we all have tendencies to
think that we did it and that we've been smart and
accomplished tremendous things, but a reality check

should quickly reveal that while we may have put a lot of effort into certain projects, it's all the Grace of God that we were able to proceed and come this far. Concerning God, "For it is he that giveth thee power to get wealth."[8] "Naked came I out of my mother's womb, and naked shall I return thither: the Lord gave, and the Lord hath taken away."[9] "The Lord maketh poor, and maketh rich."[10]

When sickness strikes often self-pity will enter. It can be a tremendous tragedy to be plagued by physical pain all the time. In such a case we will explore everything just to somehow regain our health. Certainly, there is nothing wrong with this desire. Health is a blessing and we should thank God for it every day of our lives. But if this blessing is removed for whatever reason, for a season, we shouldn't let negative thoughts enter and become bitter, but instead should turn to Jesus Christ trusting Him for the situation. Sometimes it can be difficult to relax and to trust an invisible God, when e.g. you just heard the news that you've got cancer and the doctor gives you six months to live. But even in such a case, what's really the tragic reality about such a situation? If you die indeed in six months and you're a Christian you'll be in the presence of God for the everlasting eternity. No more pain, no more problems, no more worries, but a continued celebration in Heaven throughout all eternity. Sure, the thought of leaving our loved ones behind in this terrible world is sad. But if they're Christians they'll follow us soon anyway, because, as we mentioned, these few years on earth are virtually nothing compared to the everlasting eternity. Even if we enjoy life here on earth, Heaven is a much better place to be. Not that we would ever suggest or even encourage anyone to end their physical life here on earth early by their own choice, but physical death is inevitable and if God takes us home, it isn't such a bad thing, and, in fact, is actually just another blessing.

It's important that we stress that suicide is never a solution and should never be considered, as we're not even sure where a suicide victim would spend eternity. A true Christian will be in Heaven, but nobody who commits suicide can be sure that he or she is truly a Christian. When it's time to go, God will take us home and certainly not before that appointed time. God has a plan for our lives here on earth and that's why we should look at every circumstance and problem as an opportunity—a situation that God has allowed to happen to glorify Him, which is done as we trust in Him for each situation by exercising faith in Him.

No matter what the outward circumstances and difficult situations might be, we must not panic but simply trust in Him, because the Bible asks, "Who hath hardened himself against him, and hath prospered?"[11]

Is it sin to be poor? Certainly not. Is it sin to be rich? Certainly not. Is it sin to prosper and to be blessed? Certainly not. Evidently prosperity and blessings can be misused or misapplied and that can be sin. God wants His children to be blessed and He wants them to prosper.

The blessing-and-prosperity formula, so to speak, is

thoroughly explained in the Bible. Take for example the following verse in reference to the Word of God. It says, "Meditate therein day and night, that thou mayest observe to do according to all that is written therein: for then thou shalt make thy way prosperous, and then thou shalt have good success."12 Hearing and studying the Word of God and its implementation will guarantee a prosperous life and good success. As we already explained it doesn't just mean financial prosperity, but extends to every area of life—including physical and mental health, marriage and relationships.

Regarding emotional stability it is said, that the person that makes the Word of God his delight and studies it continuously, that he or she "Shall be like a tree planted by the rivers of water, that bringeth forth his fruit in his season; his leaf also shall not wither; and whatsoever he doeth shall prosper."13 This isn't a bad promise.

God even commands a blessing whenever there is godly unity in a marriage, family, relationship, company, church, etc. You can't ask for more than to have God command a blessing. If we take in the Word of God and let the Holy Spirit work in us, it is said that "The Lord shall command the blessing upon thee in thy storehouses, and in all that thou settest thine hand unto."14 "And all these blessings shall come on thee, and overtake thee, if thou shalt hearken unto the voice of the Lord thy God. Blessed shalt thou be in the city, and blessed shalt thou be in the field. Blessed shall be the fruit of thy body, and the fruit of thy ground, and the fruit of thy cattle, the increase of thy kine, and the flocks of thy sheep. Blessed shall be thy basket and thy store. Blessed shalt thou be when thou comest in, and blessed shalt thou be when thou goest out."[15]

A self-made prosperity will always have limitations and leave us exhausted and therefore genuine happiness and fulfillment in life won't be found. While we may work hard, a divine prosperity will supply inner peace and genuine joy with supernatural energy. The self-made prosperity will always force us psychologically to hold on to its benefits, so that we don't lose any of our achievements and possessions. But a divine prosperity is full of God-given blessings and as we realize that we don't deserve these blessings, we won't have a need to protect our blessings or have a fear of losing these blessings, because God is in charge of our prosperity. Therefore we will be able to literally enjoy the blessings and we will freely share these blessings with others.

1   2 Chronicles 20:20, KJV

2   Isaiah 55:11, KJV

3   1 Timothy 6:10, KJV

4   Matthew 6:33, KJV

5   Matthew 6:21, KJV

6   3 John 2, KJV

7   "Himself" by A.B. Simpson

8   Deuteronomy 8:18, KJV

9   Job 1:21, KJV

10   1 Samuel 2:7, KJV

11   Job 9:4, KJV

12   Joshua 1:8, KJV

13   Psalm 1:3, KJV

14   Deuteronomy 28:8, KJV

15   Deuteronomy 28:2-6, KJV

PURPOSE AND GENUINE HAPPINESS

Once we understand the true purpose for our lives here on earth, depression will not even have a chance to enter anymore. Any existing condition of depression will be healed virtually instantly, because finally the purpose for our life with the proper goals and aspirations is defined. Genuine happiness will be part of our everyday lives.

What's the true purpose of life for each person? It's to get to know God and to be available to develop an intimate fellowship with Jesus Christ. As we get to know Him we will be eager to share His life with others. No longer do we have to defend our own interests or seek self-gratification and serve selfish ambitions, because our value system will be changed. Now we can be kind to others as we appreciate our own life properly. We are enabled to love others, because we're finally able to love ourselves because of the great value God has put on us and because of how much God loves us.

While man-made prosperity is in fact a hoarding procedure seeking accumulation, divine prosperity is sharing and multiplication. Outward circumstances will be unable to negatively affect and control our emotional, mental and spiritual state. Our emotions will be healthy as our mind is continuously regenerated, and our soul is cleansed and healed. During our life on earth we'll continue to be imperfect and we'll make mistakes, but by having our attitude readjusted because of our eternal destiny our life will have stability. No more pressures and haunting fears, but rather a relaxed lifestyle filled with genuine happiness, joy and peace.

"But godliness with contentment is great gain."[1] To be content doesn't mean we give up on life and seek poverty or hide in a cave, etc., but it means that we've settled the issues of life. We understand who we are and where we're going. Our purpose in life is defined. Once again, there is absolutely nothing wrong with having a career, or making a fortune in the business world, but the way it's done is now much different. You may continue to work hard, but the whole attitude is changed. Work is fun, because it's part of my life, but my job doesn't become my life. That's why such a person is content to work at a fast-food outlet, or to be the president of a multinational corporation, or for a woman to be a housewife.

Imagine all the social pressures that are all of a sudden lifted from your shoulders. If there isn't the money to buy a brand new luxury automobile maybe a used comfortable car will do. And if it can't be the mansion on the hill, the cozy little home will be just fine. Our joy is derived from a personal relationship with

Jesus Christ. As we share His life with others we're able to derive tremendous joy from this, that someone else has found Jesus Christ as their personal Savior. Every day our life can have an eternal impact and that's exciting. Some people will reject us, because of our having something they don't have and seemingly don't want to receive, even though it's available to everybody. But it's not an issue if people accept or reject us, because we've been accepted by God Himself.

"Rejoice in the Lord alway: and again I say, Rejoice."[2] Understanding this principles there is no place for depression. It's sad to see hundreds of millions of people suffer unnecessarily from depression, when there is a perfect cure for it. Making right choices doesn't hurt anyone, but makes things much easier. There are no more limitations and a genuine joy and appreciation of life will be a major benefit for the person that simply makes positive decisions. Only pride and arrogance can come in the way of letting God touch a person.

How can an ego get in the way and prevent a fulfilled life? Don't we all seek for love and peace in the home? Don't we want our marriage to work? Are we not interested in the truth? Do we not look for relief in various pressurized situations? Aren't we sick and tired of consistently complaining? Don't we want true stability and security in our life? How about real purpose and substance in our life? Do we not want to spend eternity in the presence of God? Do we really think that our few years on earth are really everything there is to life? Are we so deceived and blinded that we can't see and find truth anymore? Do we have to prove to society that we're really worth something by playing their game according to their rules? Do we have to accept the world's solutions to problems which the world created and imposed on us in the first place?

It's a fact that we're living in an imperfect world with imperfect people and not every experience in life is a pleasant one. There are hostile attacks and severe tragedies. But in all of this there is hope (hope = confident expectation) based on objective truth that we can deal with all of that victoriously and with inner peace and tremendous joy. Depression is not a solution. The solution to being healed from the devastating cycles of depression is to draw near to God by simply meditating on His Word after receiving Jesus Christ as personal Savior. Let's sit down and consider what was said in this book step by step. Crucial details were analyzed and explained. The absolutely most effective solution and cure for depression was provided and explained—it's valid for everybody. It's up to us to accept it or reject it. Do you still think that there is something better? Considering everything, I'm sure that there isn't anything better. Some philosophies and concepts may sound better or may seem initially better, but they aren't.

Whenever I suffered so severely from depression at an early age, I wasn't sent to a psychiatrist nor did I receive medication for my condition. It's a miracle that I survived these vicious cycles of depression which lasted for nearly a decade. It's also a miracle that I've been completely healed from depression not by medication, or by psychological counsel from secular people, but purely by the power of the Word of God and the working of the Holy Spirit. This "treatment" is available to everybody and we've seen it work effectively thousands of times over the years.

We've also seen people that have rejected this Word of God "treatment" and instead continued to pursue healing from depression by medication and secular counsel. We're unable to see permanent results of healing in these people, because these people continue to live consistently on the edge and verge of suicide. Bitterness is settled deeply within them, along with undefined anger and never being able to experience genuine happiness. They seemingly have no real purpose in their life and no hope so to speak. There is just a plain meaningless existence which doesn't benefit themselves nor anyone else. Sad, and we certainly don't want to leave you with this lugubrious scenario.

Simply one positive choice towards God and a life can be changed in a moment. For practical application, at first receive Jesus Christ as your personal Savior. Follow this by purchasing a quality Study Bible and finding a Bible-believing local church. At the local church you'll meet people that have the same interest in spiritual matters as you have. In the Study Bible read the various themes that are of interest to you—usually found in the back of your Bible—and that's how you can learn about the mind of Christ. If you have never read a Bible before or only read it casually it's best to start in the New Testament with the gospel recorded by John.

The Psalms are always very encouraging and helpful as explained earlier in this book. After the Psalms there are the Proverbs of King Solomon which contain a lot of wisdom for practical application in everyday life. Needless to say, all of the Bible is beneficial and edifying, but it doesn't make much sense in the beginning to just read it from cover to cover. It's better to study the Word of God in categories and subjects, here a little and there a little. Listen to the Word of God preached by the pastor of your local Bible-believing church, which will enlighten you even more.

If possible read this book a few times, or certain topics that speak to you specifically, because this can be very helpful. We encourage you to accept and follow the advice and suggestions provided in this book and I'm sure they'll help you. Do not accept any kind of negativity or pessimism about yourself, your work, your behavior, etc. Try to get on a strict diet of positive communication including in your thought life. Practice the "I love me" principle knowing that God loves you so much and you're truly very special. I would not have written this book if I didn't care about you in particular. The Bible says in referring to every Christian that we are "members in particular"3—meaning we can rest assured that God really cares for each individual very specifically and He is very well aware of what we're going through.

Positive communication is very important, because it keeps depression away. There is always something positive that we can focus on and that we can find. Avoid arguing, because nobody wins and it is destructive. We don't always need to be right, but we can bring our concerns to God and ask Him to bring healing to a situation. It is not seldom that a person is misunderstood and it happens to every individual. We don't need to get angry because of that. Don't worry about certain habits if they don't go away immediately—these things are not the issue and I firmly believe that the intake of the Word of God through the power of the Holy Spirit can eliminate bad habits eventually.

Regarding certain issues, we have to make certain decisions in order to experience the consequences and benefits of right choices. Sometimes we just have to let go of things in order to receive something much better. Overall, it's certainly not a self-help program, but rather a new arrangement of priorities and thoughts. It's not difficult to do that, especially if we trust God for doing it for us the whole experience is a daily adventure. Once things are in motion you'll like it a lot, because life all of a sudden looks different. Many problems are no longer problems, and you'll enjoy more and more days of genuine happiness, relaxation and the sense of a rich, purposeful life with real significance. Your life will have an eternal impact and produce eternal results in the lives of many other people.

You finally will be happy with who you are and you'll love yourself. Some things you may not like about yourself, but the positive aspects of your life will overwhelm all these little nasty things, so that you're free from the bondage of these things, and are able to live a victorious life. Your life will be a testimony to others of how great life can really be aside from outward circumstances. Inner peace and joy many people don't have, but you will have it. Circumstances and certain situations always reveal if people truly operate in wisdom and trust in God.

There will always be situations that give us a choice to react just as people would expect us to react, or to respond to a situation within the realm of divine attributes and objectivity. We can always panic and exalt our ego and choose to react and let it rip so to speak, but nobody is going to benefit from a destructive game of intimidation. How about some mercy and grace? Situations can dramatically change for the better by a kind approach. Even though at times a kind and peaceful approach isn't considered "professional" it still is the better approach, which will ultimately benefit all parties involved. Thinking of the business world, it's sick to hear that so and so is suing so and so, and years are being wasted in hate and retaliation. There are, of course, certain legitimate situations to participate in a court battle, in cases of a crime, etc., but just to prove a point or to intimidate someone because of greed is certainly no grounds for a legal battle.

When do people realize that life isn't fair? If life is fair or not isn't the issue. God is just and He loves everyone and we have an opportunity to have a close personal relationship and even intimate fellowship with Him. Obviously God knows everything and He knows when we're wronged, and He looks at the choice we make of either reaction or response. Based on the decisions we make, He can reward us and bless us tremendously, even in the worst and most hopeless situations.

Every person that is honest to themselves has no reason whatsoever to be depressed. Especially living in the civilized world where there is an abundance of food, shelter and economic opportunities everywhere, there are no reasons to enter into a cycle of depression, unless a person is absolutely selfish and doesn't want to be helped. Frustration can happen at times, but doesn't need to lead to depression if dealt with appropriately.

If you're truly caught up in a physically abusive relationship you should get counsel immediately. If counsel doesn't work within a short period of time, at least a separation for the time being might be necessary so that the offending party is able to receive treatment. If things don't change such a relationship must be terminated in order to protect your own life and perhaps the lives of your children. While these situations are sad, these things are no reason to let yourself be dragged down and enter into depression. Maybe you want to examine your conduct, too. Maybe your behavior is provocative, which could be the case. If the woman keeps on nagging and not doing her work in the home, and is consistently demanding this and that, this puts a lot of pressure on the husband. Try some kindness and love, and if it doesn't work you've got to take action as mentioned above.

If you're lonely and perhaps you don't have any meaningful relationships, it's time for you to establish an intimate relationship with Jesus Christ. Let Him heal you and lead you and provide you with meaningful relationships. If you're physically ill, don't give up, God can heal you at any moment, but don't let your desire for healing become a demand and your utmost concern. God's plan is perfect, even though we may not understand it. He is a gracious God and He hears our prayers. Every day and every hour is a gift from God and it's another opportunity to get to know Him. The only thing that will count in eternity is how much I took hold of opportunities to get to know Him.

"Blessed be the Lord, who daily loadeth us with benefits."[4] He has equipped us to live meaningful and fruitful lives with purpose here on earth. We can make our lives count and have significance as we make eternal impacts. Others must hear the truth and we can be part of this process of sharing Him with others, "And he that winneth souls is wise."[5] We're wise if we share the gospel of Jesus Christ with others. Listen to what happens to the individuals who are wise according to God's standard, "And they that be wise shall shine as the brightness of the firmament; and they that turn many to righteousness, as the stars for ever and ever."[6]

This life is available to everybody, to whosoever will accept it. It's a victorious life with phenomenal inward joy, great purpose and powerful substance. Imagine to just speak a word or a silent prayer and mountains can be moved. Every thought counts and every word we speak can have an eternal effect. Considering all of this, there is certainly no place for depression. These thoughts alone could bring immediate healing to the receptive soul. Life is great. Life is beautiful. Life is a gift from God. There is no place for depression. If people would like to, everybody could overcome depression, and most certainly everybody can avoid depression—it's not difficult. God does it for us if we let Him. This requires simply the positive agreeing of our free volition with His Word. Enjoy life and let your life be a celebration of life. Let's shine as the stars forever and ever—your life counts and it is very important. God bless!

1   1 Timothy 6:6, KJV

2   Philippians 4:4, KJV

3   1 Corinthians 12:27, KJV

4   Psalm 68:19, KJV

5   Proverbs 11:30, KJV

6   Daniel 12:3, KJV

ABOUT THE AUTHOR

Born into a poverty-stricken family in June of 1961, Dietmar Scherf grew up in Graz, Austria. His parents were hard-working folks and it took them a few years to leave their moist two-room living quarters in a basement behind. Finally, they moved into a small, but new and clean apartment during the mid-sixties.

Plagued with depression and seeds of suicide he barely survived his teenage years in his working-class environment. In 1976, he began studying human behavior. His interest in business required the study of sales and marketing psychology to discover and understand the laws of cause and effect, and the herd mentality.

In search for adventure, he left Austria at the age of eighteen and traveled the United States and Europe for almost two years. The early eighties were once again a time of various studies. While business and psychology were always of great interest to Dietmar Scherf, a new vital addition of extensive studies began for him in late 1980—Christianity. Having been raised a Roman Catholic, he also studied various religions in the late seventies. And in 1980, he became a born-again Christian which changed his life forever. His studies in the Word of God began to intensify in 1982, and after a few years he was completely healed from depression. Revived with a new outlook for life he married in the spring of 1987. Applying spiritual principles and godly wisdom by the Grace of God, he enjoyed the outpouring of tremendous blessings and Dietmar Scherf became a celebrity in his native country of Austria by 1989. Even though not forgotten, but gone were the suicidal depressive moods from a decade earlier. A great physical healing also took place in Dietmar's life in 1985.

Having evolved to be a renowned sales and marketing psychologist and being a guest speaker at universities and special events in Austria, in the early nineties, Dietmar Scherf became more and more in demand by companies and individuals in the U.S. and Europe as a valuable consultant. In 1990, Dietmar Scherf made the United States his new home and appeared frequently as a featured guest speaker at various business and company meetings, in schools, on talk-radio, and at churches. In 1996, Dietmar Scherf moved his family from Bel Air, Maryland to fabulous Las Vegas, Nevada.

ACKNOWLEDGMENTS

It is my absolute obligation to thank especially Dr. Carl H. Stevens for his consistent and loving encouragement in presenting objective truth in season and out of season for the over 15 years that I've known him so far. If it wasn't for his teaching and his living example of practical application of what he taught, I would never have been able to understand and present the insight, pertaining to this subject, revealed in this book in depth. He's also been a rare true friend for many years.

I'm also indebted to Dr. Daniel E. Lewis whose communication of specific wisdom for specific situations and his real-life applications of such wisdom has truly protected me from much foolishness over the years.

Special thanks to Pastor Bill Reed. I am also grateful to Barbara Dague and Nicole Rodriguez.

Certainly, all of this and everything else has only been made possible by the amazing Grace of God. Our Lord and Savior Jesus Christ has never and will never let us down. His Word will stand forever.

RECOMMENDED READINGS

THE BIBLE

In order to study the Word of God in specific categories and topics, a very good Study Bible is necessary. The Thompson Chain-Reference® Bible will be extensive. The Ryrie Study Bible is also recommended. Regarding English translations of the Bible, the King James Version continues to be a very good translation, even though it doesn't use a contemporary English. The New American Standard Bible is also a very good translation and it uses a contemporary English. To investigate the original text of the Bible, The Amplified Bible is an excellent study tool and is a great addition. These Bibles can be purchased at most Christian bookstores and in some regular bookstores. An excellent source to purchase Bibles at a discount is CBD (Christian Book Distributors). To request a catalog from CBD (Christian Book Distributors) call Tel. (978) 977-5000 or write to: CBD, P.O. Box 7000, Peabody, MA 01961-7000, USA

SPIRITUAL LITERATURE

Grace Publications publishes one booklet a week on a specific spiritual category. Most of these booklets are compiled from messages by Dr. Carl H. Stevens, who has been teaching the Word of God for over 40 years. He is an expert in his field. To request information about the publishing program of Grace Publications, call Telephone (410) 483-3700 or write to: Grace Publications, P.O. Box 18715, Baltimore, MD 21206, USA

MEET WITH DIETMAR SCHERF IN PERSON

Mr. Scherf continues to be an occasional guest speaker at various events. It's always an exciting experience when he travels the country to speak at seminars, conventions, church services, etc. If you like to meet with Mr. Scherf in person to hear him speak, then please send a postcard or note with your name and address written legibly to our address (Attn: Free Info) to receive a free schedule of speaking engagements.

*[Companies, Churches, Organizations, etc. interested in having Mr. Scherf speak at their event may contact Scherf, Inc. to obtain a fee schedule and to inquire about availability of date(s). In order to process your inquiry promptly, please indicate the following basic details: **(A)** Describe briefly who you are and what the nature of your company's business is, or the cause of your organization; **(B)** Desired date for the speaking engagement with optional choice of other dates if any. Please also indicate location of event; **(C)** Brief description of the scheduled event, e.g. company motivational meeting, or charitable event to benefit a certain cause or group, etc. including the theme of the event if any. Please also indicate if Mr. Scherf will be featured as the sole guest speaker, or together with other speakers at a seminar, church service, etc.; **(D)** Approximate size of expected audience; **(E)** Other relevant information that may help us to process your request efficaciously.]*

OTHER BOOKS BY
DIETMAR SCHERF

Since 1983, a combined total of over a hundred articles, research reports and booklets by Dietmar Scherf on various subjects have been published. Currently, he is working on several unique, inspiring and very exciting novels, which are scheduled to be published during the coming years. Check with your local bookstore periodically or write to us and we'll send you free information regarding new releases of new books by Dietmar Scherf. To receive free information please simply send a postcard or note with your name and address written legibly to our address (Attn: Free Info).

RELAXED MUSIC

Now you can enjoy relaxed instrumental music composed and performed by Dietmar Scherf. *"Nice To Meet Ya!"* is a unique musical journey consisting of upbeat contemporary background music for daydreamers. Many musical compositions on this CD have been used for relaxed exercise workouts and as driving music for long and short trips. Almost a full hour (59:48) of absolute relaxation. *"Nice To Meet Ya!"* is only available on Compact Disc (CD). The price of each CD is only US$15. To order this CD please use or copy the Order Form in the back of this book and fill out legibly, and send it with your full payment to our address indicated on the Order Form (Free S&H in the U.S. and worldwide!).

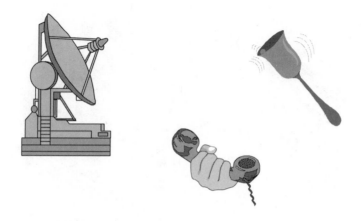

SPREADING THE NEWS

After reading this book, you perhaps like other people to read *"I Love Me • Avoiding & Overcoming Depression."* It's really a "Must-read" for everybody. This book makes a great and valuable gift for every occasion and each recipient will be thankful and grateful to you for choosing such an excellent gift. To spread the news simply tell your friends and neighbors about this book. Buy additional copies of this book at your local bookstore, or order directly from *SCHERF BOOKS.* Please use or copy the Order Form in the back of this book and fill out legibly, and send it with your full payment to our address indicated on the Order Form (Free S&H in the U.S. and worldwide!).

ORGANIZING SCHERF MEETINGS

Another great way of spreading the news and having fun doing it, is to arrange and organize a meeting/seminar with Dietmar Scherf as the guest speaker in your area. You can do this yourself or together with your friends and neighbors. Depending on how you go about arranging such a meeting, you could even earn an extra income of up to several thousand dollars.

These meetings will help your community and every attending person in many different ways. It will be certainly a very satisfying experience of truly helping a lot of people. If you are a gifted organizer and already have detailed plans to organize a Scherf Meeting in your area, please contact our office for availability of dates and regarding some information of basic logistics.

ORDER FORM
(Copy or use this Original)

Item Description	Qty.	Each	Total
I LOVE ME • Avoiding & Overcoming Depression		**$22**	$
Music CD•Nice To Meet Ya!		$15	$
FREE S&H in U.S. & International			
TOTAL US$			

FREE S&H worldwide! **RUSH DELIVERY GUARANTEED!**
(Priority shipment is immediately made. Personal checks must clear before order is shipped. All sales final.)

US$ funds only drawn on a bank in USA.

Send Check or
Money Order to: **SCHERF**
PO BOX 80180
LAS VEGAS, NV 89180-0180
USA

Credit Card (Visa/MC) Orders:

Credit Card Number: _____

Expiration Date: _____/_____
                          Signature: _____

Name_____

Address_____

City_____

State_____ ZIP _____